Cutscores: A Manual for Setting Standards of Performance on Educational and Occupational Tests

Michael J. Zieky
Educational Testing Service

Marianne Perie
National Center for the Improvement
of Educational Assessment, Inc.

Samuel A. Livingston
Educational Testing Service

We wish to thank our reviewers: Charles DePascale, Carol Dwyer, Daniel Eignor, Ronald Hambleton, Michael Kane, Stephen Lazer, Mary Pitoniak, Barbara Plake, W. James Popham, and Richard Tannenbaum. We appreciate their willingness to share their wisdom, knowledge, and experience with us. Any remaining flaws are the responsibility of the authors. We also wish to thank William Monaghan, the editor and compositor of this manual.

The views expressed in this manual are those of the authors and not necessarily those of our reviewers, ETS or NCIEA.

Educational Testing Service (ETS) is a nonprofit institution with the mission to advance quality and equity in education by providing fair and valid assessments, research and related services for all people worldwide. For more information about ETS, visit the organization's Web site, *www.ets.org.*

The National Center for the Improvement of Educational Assessment, Inc. (NCIEA) was founded to contribute to improved student achievement through enhanced practices in educational assessment and accountability. More information can be found at the Web site, *www.nciea.org.*

 *Listening. Learning. Leading*®

 The National Center for the Improvement of Educational Assessment, Inc.

TABLE OF CONTENTS

1. INTRODUCTION

1.1 Purpose and Intended Readers

This manual is about setting cutscores.[1] A cutscore is a point on a test's score scale used to determine whether or not a particular test score is sufficient for some purpose. For example, test takers with scores at or above the cutscore on a licensing test are awarded a license to practice a profession. Test takers below that point are denied a license. Test takers with scores at or above a certain cutscore on an educational accountability test

> **This is a how-to-do-it manual aimed at people who have to plan and run a cutscore study.**

are classified as Proficient. Test takers with scores below the Proficient point are classified as Basic. There may be more than one cutscore on a test. For example, a cutscore above the Proficient point may be used to distinguish between test takers who are Proficient and test takers who are Advanced.

We wrote this manual for people who have to set cutscores on educational or occupational tests, but who are not sure what to do.[2] This is a how-to-do-it manual aimed at people who have to plan and run a cutscore study. It has more detail than policymakers need and none of the scholarly references in the text that graduate students and researchers want. There are no formulas or statistical symbols. Our focus is on practical advice rather than on theory or reviews of research. We want to tell you what we now wish we had known about setting cutscores when we first started helping people to set them.

The manual is at a level of detail that will help you to select a method for setting cutscores and then apply that method, step by step. We assume that you are not a statistician and that you

---

[1] Many authors use the word *standards* to refer to cutscores. We prefer *cutscores* because *standards* has other important meanings as in, for example, the *Standards for Educational and Psychological Testing*. We used to prefer the term *passing scores,* but cutscores are now used for many performance levels in addition to pass and fail.

[2] Strictly speaking, only people with the legal authority to do so, such as policymakers, can set operational cutscores. We will, however, follow common usage and talk about what you do when you set cutscores, even if you are not a policymaker.

are not a measurement specialist. We also assume that you have had no prior experience in setting cutscores. You do not need to have any specialized knowledge to use this manual, but you will need the help of a statistician who is familiar with educational measurement to use some of the methods we describe for setting cutscores. We will let you know when you will need the statistician's help.

Most of our experiences with cutscores have been in the United States, and the examples used in this manual reflect those experiences. The concepts discussed in this manual, however, apply wherever cutscores are used.

1.2 Background

This manual is an update of *Passing Scores: A Manual for Setting Standards of Performance on Educational and Occupational Tests,* which was written by two of us (Livingston and Zieky), and published by Educational Testing Service in 1982. *Passing Scores* is still a useful document and we have freely used both verbatim and slightly revised excerpts from it.

We decided to update *Passing Scores* because much has changed in the setting and uses of cutscores in the quarter century since the manual was first published. In the early 1980s, cutscores were used primarily on licensing tests for occupations and on high school exit tests that measured basic skills. Those tests consisted almost entirely of multiple-choice questions, and the cutscore was used to distinguish only between passing and failing scores.

In the last 25 years, there has been much research on setting cutscores. New methods of setting cutscores have been invented and have become very popular. In addition, some components of procedures for setting cutscores that were once considered optional have grown in importance and have become common practice. These include sharing normative information on test taker performance with the participants in a cutscore study, having several iterations of judgments during the study, and encouraging the participants to discuss their judgments between those iterations. Documentation requirements for cutscore studies have become much more rigorous, and attempts to evaluate cutscores have become more widespread. New controversies have arisen. Some prominent researchers have characterized several commonly used methods of setting cutscores as "fundamentally flawed" because of their concerns about the difficulty of making the required judgments, and other researchers have vigorously defended those methods.

The use of cutscores in schools increased throughout the 1970s, the 1980s and the 1990s to support the growth of criterion referenced testing, the basic skills testing movement, and standards-based education reform. The use of cutscores surged in the early 21st century when the *No Child Left Behind* Act of 2001 (NCLB) became a law in the United States. In an effort to increase accountability for the results of elementary and secondary education, NCLB required all states to have assessments in reading and mathematics at each of

> *The use of cutscores in schools increased throughout the 1970s, the 1980s and the 1990s to support the growth of criterion referenced testing, the basic skills testing movement, and standards-based education reform.*

grades 3–8 and once in high school. Science tests are required in at least one grade in each of three grade ranges: 3–5, 6–9, and 10–12. NCLB mandates a minimum of three performance levels: one indicating Proficient performance, one indicating performance above Proficient, often termed Advanced, and one indicating performance below Proficient, often termed Basic.

In the K–12 education system, the emphasis has moved from setting a single cutscore that differentiates between Pass and Fail to setting multiple cutscores that differentiate among several levels of knowledge and skills. Those cutscores have to be aligned across grades in reasonable ways. For example, the Proficient cutscore in grade 4 reading must indicate a higher level of performance than the Proficient cutscore in grade 3 reading. Finally, many of the tests currently used include constructed-response (e.g., essay) questions as well as selected-response (e.g., multiple-choice) questions. New methods of setting cutscores have been designed to integrate judgments about both types of questions when they are used in the same test.

Even though much has been written about cutscores, the research on setting cutscores does not yet provide definitive answers to many important questions. Decisions about how to select and run a cutscore study often depend on opinions rather than data. Opinions about many aspects of setting cutscores still differ among researchers and among practitioners (and among the authors of this manual). We believe, however, that we are in sufficient agreement on many important issues to share our opinions with you and to make some specific recommendations about how to plan and conduct cutscore studies.

Because this is a how-to-do-it manual, we decided not to burden the text with references to the professional literature on setting cutscores each time we describe a method, state a fact or make a specific recommendation. We do not wish to give the impression, however, that we originated all of the information contained in this manual by ourselves. We owe much to our colleagues who freely shared their knowledge at conferences and in their publications. In the section devoted to methods, we acknowledge the authors associated with the methods of setting cutscores that we describe. We would like to acknowledge here several people whose writings and presentations have been the source of much of our general knowledge about cutscores: Ronald A. Berk, Mary Lyn Bourque, Gregory J. Cizek, Ronald K. Hambleton, James C. Impara, Richard M. Jaeger, Michael T. Kane, Susan C. Loomis, Craig N. Mills, Mary J. Pitoniak, Barbara S. Plake, W. James Popham, Mark D. Reckase, and Lorrie A. Shepard.

1.3 Overview

There are ten narrative sections in this manual plus suggestions for further reading, a glossary, and an appendix.

1. Introduction

   This brief section, which you are reading now, contains an explanation of our purpose in writing the manual, a description of the intended readers, some background information, and an overview of the contents of the manual.

2. What You Should Know About Cutscores

   We believe that setting cutscores is not just a mechanical task. We think that you can do a better job of setting cutscores if you understand their characteristics. Therefore, this section defines cutscores as decision rules, stresses the judgmental nature of cutscores, describes the two types of misclassifications that occur when you use cutscores, discusses the relative harm caused by each type of misclassification, and describes the appropriate uses of data when you set cutscores.

3. What You Have to Do Before You Set Cutscores

Preparing for a cutscore study involves many complicated steps and critical decisions. Lack of preparation is likely to cause severe problems. This section describes the important things you should do before you set cutscores, regardless of the method that you will use. You will have to plan the cutscore study, decide whether to use a cutscore on the total test or separate cutscores on subscores, define performance levels, write performance level descriptors, select a method, decide how to apply the method, obtain staff and facilities, select participants, train participants, define borderline performance, and comply with professional standards.

4. Overviews of Methods of Setting Cutscores

This section contains general descriptions of some useful methods of setting cutscores. We describe the following methods:

- Angoff method
- Angoff Mean Estimation method
- Angoff Yes or No method
- Nedelsky method
- Ebel method
- Bookmark method
- Item Descriptor Matching method
- Performance Profile method
- Dominant Profile method
- Borderline Group method
- Contrasting Groups method
- Up and Down Modification of the Contrasting Groups method
- Body of Work method
- Analytic Judgment method
- Single Reference Group method
- Two Reference Groups method
- Beuk method
- Hofstee method

This section also includes descriptions of the advantages and disadvantages of using each method. We suggest that you read the overviews of all of the methods to get an idea of the possibilities available to you for setting cutscores, and choose a method as described in section 5, before you read about the procedural details of any particular method in section 6.

5. How to Choose a Method

This section contains decision rules to help you select the methods that are appropriate for your particular circumstances. We offer advice to help you decide which method to select.

6. Detailed Procedures for Setting Cutscores

This section contains detailed, step-by-step procedures for setting cutscores by each of the methods described in section 4. After you have selected a method to use, you will need to read the detailed procedures for that method. If the procedures for the method you have chosen refer to the procedures for another method described earlier, you will also have to read the procedures for the referenced method. Feel free to skip the detailed procedures for the methods in which you have no interest.

7. What You Have to Do After You Set Cutscores

Your task is not completed at the end of the cutscore study. This section describes the important things you should do after the cutscore study, such as reviewing and documenting the study, and evaluating the cutscores.

8. Tips

Lots of things can go wrong in a cutscore study. This section contains tips to help you to avoid problems and to help you deal with the problems that you cannot avoid. The section includes information about planning a cutscore study, preparing materials, running the study, dealing with common problems, and answering frequently asked questions.

9. Consistency Across Grades

Cutscores are now commonly used across a number of consecutive school grades in the United States. You should read this section if you want advice on the relatively new problem of obtaining reasonably consistent cutscores across grade levels.

10. Conclusion

This very brief section offers a few final thoughts to keep in mind as you set cutscores.

Further Reading

This part of the manual contains references to chapters, books and articles that will help you learn more about setting cutscores than we could include in this manual. We have included references for each method we discuss as well as documents of general interest.

Glossary

This part of the manual contains definitions of the specialized terminology that we used regarding measurement and cutscores.

Appendix

This part of the manual contains samples of some of the forms that are used at cutscore meetings.

2. WHAT YOU SHOULD KNOW ABOUT CUTSCORES

There are some fundamental truths about cutscores that you should understand before you try to set cutscores. The following facts apply to all cutscores, regardless of the methods used to set them.

2.1 A Cutscore Is a Decision Rule

A test score is a piece of information about a person. What is the best way to use that information to make a decision? Can you make better decisions based on tests if you use cutscores, or can you make better decisions without using cutscores?

In many situations, cutscores are not necessary. Cutscores are not needed for norm-referenced interpretations of scores in which a test taker's score is given meaning by comparisons with the scores of some group of test takers. For example, a score could be given meaning by saying that it represented performance in reading that was better than the performance of 90 percent of the fifth grade students in the United States.

If a test is being used to allocate a fixed number of opportunities, choosing a cutscore is not necessary. If the opportunities are to go to the most able, you can simply count down from the top of the score distribution until all of the available openings are filled. If the opportunities are to go to the neediest, you can simply count up from the bottom.

If, however, the test is used to determine which people have enough knowledge and skills to be qualified for some particular purpose, simply counting down from the top, or up from the bottom will not work. It is possible that even the highest-scoring test takers are not qualified, or that even the lowest-scoring test takers are qualified. How should you decide which test takers are qualified?

One way to decide is to consider each person's test score plus whatever other information you like, apply your own judgment, and make the decision. This case-by-case method of decision-making has some important advantages. It offers you the chance to consider each test taker individually on the basis of all the information available to you, whether you had planned to use it in advance, or not. Case-by-case decision-making allows you to use different information for different test takers. It allows you to treat test takers with the same scores differently. The decisions about test takers are not constrained by consistent rules.

Case-by-case decision-making has some serious drawbacks, however. Two different decision-makers can arrive at different decisions on the basis of the same information. You cannot adequately describe the criteria for your decisions in the form of a statement to the test takers and other interested persons. If people accuse you of being inconsistent, you cannot claim that you were following the same rules for all test takers. In short, case-by-case decision-making offers no assurance that test takers will be treated fairly. As a result, it can leave you open to charges of favoritism or prejudice.

You may, therefore, prefer to use a *decision rule* that you will apply in the same way to all test takers. Your decision rule will specify what information you will use and how you will use it in making decisions about individual test takers. One common type of decision rule is to use cutscores to classify the test takers into groups based on their test scores. Often, the decision rule combines test scores with other information. For example, a professional certification board might grant certification only to persons who have completed an accredited training program, have at least two years' experience in the profession, and earn at least a specified score on a test.

2.2 Cutscores Depend on Judgments

All cutscores are based on judgment. There is no way to avoid judgment when you set a cutscore. Every method of setting cutscores depends on judgment at some point in the process. (The redundancy is intentional. We want to make this point as strongly as possible. Knowing that cutscores are based on judgment is fundamental to understanding cutscores and the methods for setting them.)

All cutscores are based on judgment.

Some people have criticized the use of cutscores on educational and occupational tests because the cutscores are based on judgments, without realizing that cutscores based on judgments are common and useful in many important aspects of life. Cutscores based on judgments specify the minimum amount of butterfat required in whole milk, the largest acceptable number of coliform bacteria per milliliter in municipal drinking water, the minimum voting age, and the distinction between normal blood pressure and high blood pressure. The fact that cutscores are based on judgments does not make it wrong to use cutscores in any field, including educational and occupational testing. We think you should use cutscores whenever they can help you make better decisions.

> *Your job is to choose the cutscores by a method that is based on judgments that can be made meaningfully and realistically, to select participants who are qualified to make those judgments, and to provide the information the participants need to make those judgments wisely.*

Your job in setting cutscores is not to avoid judgments. Your job is to choose the cutscores by a method that is based on judgments that can be made meaningfully and realistically, to select participants who are qualified to make those judgments, and to provide the information the participants need to make those judgments wisely. We will discuss how to do those things in later sections of this manual.

2.3 There Is No True Cutscore

Your job is not to find the one, true, perfect cutscore. There is no such thing. To understand why not, consider the difference between deciding how tall a particular police officer is and deciding what the minimum height for a police officer should be. If several people measured the height of a particular police officer, there would be some small variation in their results. This variation might be caused by slight differences in their measuring techniques and in the way the officer was standing. If they took the measurements at different times of day, there would be some variation caused by the tendency of people to be slightly shorter late in the day (because their spinal discs compress). But you could specify a set of rules for determining which measurements had been made correctly, and you could then consider the average of all those measurements as the officer's "true" height.

Determining the minimum height that should be required for police officers is a very different problem. People's judgments of the minimum required height will depend on their view of the various tasks a police officer must do and on the extent to which they believe the officer's height affects the performance of those tasks. Specifying the minimum required height for all officers is a matter of subjective judgment, in a way that measuring the height of an individual officer is not.

In educational and occupational testing, there is no true cutscore that could be discovered if only the perfect method could be perfectly implemented. The cutscore is determined by the people who set it. The number that is obtained from a cutscore study depends on the experiences, values and beliefs of the people who served as participants in the cutscore study. It also depends on such factors as the particular method used to set the cutscore and the way that the method is implemented by a particular facilitator (the person in charge of running the cutscore study). A change in any of these factors would be likely to result in a different cutscore. Consequently, there is no single right answer to the question, "What should the cutscore be for this test?"

> *...there is no true cutscore that could be discovered if only the perfect method could be perfectly implemented.*

How much is the cutscore likely to change if you use a different method to set the cutscore, or use the same method with different participants? To determine the extent to which the cutscore would change with a different method, you actually have to use two or more methods. But you may be able to determine the extent to which the cutscore would change with different participants, if you use a method that produces a separate cutscore for each participant. In that case, your statistician will be able to compute statistics from a single study that indicate (based on certain assumptions) how much the cutscore would tend to vary from one sample of participants to another, if all the other factors (method, facilitator, etc.) remained the same.

You will not be able to find the one true cutscore, but we hope that the information and advice in this manual will enable you to construct a reasonable cutscore, using a generally accepted method that you have implemented correctly.

2.4 There Will Be Misclassifications

No matter how well you set the cutscore, some test takers are likely to be misclassified (placed in the wrong category).[3] The test scores of any sizable group of test takers tend to be distributed without meaningful gaps, because the knowledge and skills that are being tested tend to be distributed without gaps. People who score close to each other on a test tend to be very similar in their levels of the knowledge and skills that are being tested. Yet when you set a cutscore, people who just reach the cutscore will be classified differently, and may be treated very differently, than people who score one point lower.

> *No matter how well you set the cutscore, some test takers are likely to be misclassified (placed in the wrong category).*

On some tests, being above or below a cutscore can make a big difference in a person's life. But for a test taker whose true ability is very close to the level indicated by the cutscore, earning a score just above the cutscore or a score just below it may depend heavily on chance. For example, suppose that a testing program administers several different forms of a test in a year. Even if all those test forms are equally difficult for the group of test takers as a whole, an individual test taker's score will depend somewhat on the particular questions on the form of the test that happens to be administered to that test taker. For example, a test taker who is an avid photographer may happen to be given a form of the test that has a reading passage about photography.

For some test takers, good luck or bad luck in guessing an answer or two may determine whether they score above or below the cutscore. If subjectively scored constructed-response questions, such as essays, are used on the test, the severity of the scorers who happen to be selected to read the test taker's responses may determine whether the test taker scores above or below the cutscore. In short, no test is perfectly reliable (i.e.,

---

[3] In the discussion of misclassifications we will use the terms *pass* and *fail* because they are easy to understand in this context. The same logic holds, however, for any classifications made on the basis of cutscores such as Basic and Proficient.

completely unaffected by chance factors). A test taker whose ability is close to the level represented by the cutscore may pass or fail because of chance factors.

Furthermore, no test is perfectly valid (measuring everything that should be measured and nothing that should not be measured). A test taker whose ability is just above the cutscore in the skills the test is *intended* to measure may have abilities just below the cutscore in some of the other skills the test *actually* measures. For example, a student whose reading skills are weak may fail a test of science knowledge, even though her knowledge of the subject is adequate, if her weak reading skills cause her to misunderstand several of the test questions.

> *Avoiding cutscores does not allow you to avoid misclassifications. The only way to avoid misclassifications entirely is to avoid making any classifications.*

Therefore it is probable that some people who should pass will fail, and some people who should fail will pass. These misclassifications will happen even if everything is done well in test development, test administration, and test scoring. Good test development practices, good test administration practices, and good test scoring practices can reduce the number of misclassifications, but cannot eliminate them entirely.

Please keep in mind that, no matter how you make classification decisions about people, you will make some misclassifications. Avoiding cutscores does not allow you to avoid misclassifications. The only way to avoid misclassifications entirely is to avoid making any classifications.

2.5 Some Misclassifications Are More Harmful than Others

If you raise the cutscore, people who should fail will be less likely to pass. But people who should pass will be more likely to fail. If you lower the cutscore, people who should pass will be less likely to fail. But people who should fail will be more likely to pass. You can reduce one type of misclassification by raising or lowering the cutscore, but doing so will increase the other type of misclassification. Therefore, an important consideration in setting cutscores is to decide which type of misclassification is worse than the other, and how much worse it is.

In some cases, most people would agree that one type of misclassification is worse than another. For example, most people would agree that on a test used to license air traffic controllers, it is more harmful to pass a test taker who should fail than it would be to fail a test taker who should pass. Even in that situation, however, people might disagree about *how much* worse it would be. For example, some people might believe that denying licenses to aspiring controllers will increase the workload of the controllers already on the job, possibly causing them to work less effectively. How bad is it to pass one test taker who should fail? Is it as bad as failing two who should pass? As bad as failing three who should pass? Five? Ten? Twenty?

To further complicate the matter, not all misclassifications of the same type are equally harmful. For example, if the cutscore on the air traffic controller's test is 72, passing a test taker whose true ability would correspond to a score of 70 is not as harmful as passing a test taker whose true ability would correspond to a score of 36.

In most academic situations, people disagree even about which type of misclassification is worse. For example, people tend to disagree about whether it is worse to misclassify a student who is only Proficient in fifth-grade reading as Advanced, or to misclassify a student who is truly Advanced as Proficient.

If either type of misclassification caused no harm, you would not need to use a test with a cutscore. You could simply pass everybody or fail everybody. For example, if passing a test taker who really should fail would do no harm at all, your best decision rule would be to pass everybody. When you set cutscores, take *both* types of possible misclassifications into account.

You will probably need to explain the inevitability of misclassifications to the participants in your cutscore study. Make sure they understand that reducing one type of misclassification increases the other type of misclassification, and help them think about which type of misclassification is worse and how much worse it is.

2.6 Normative Information Is Useful

When criterion referenced testing[4] was still novel, its adherents emphasized how different it was from the then much more common norm-referenced testing. Some of the early users of criterion referenced testing argued against the use of normative information in setting cutscores. They believed that normative information, such as the difficulty of test questions or the percent of test takers who would pass, would "contaminate" the process of deciding what test takers should know and be able to do.

We believe that the judgments of participants in a cutscore study are heavily influenced by whatever normative information they happen to have internalized about what people know and can do. Some participants, such as a teacher from a highly selective school, may be familiar primarily with atypical test takers. Some participants may be depending on outdated information, and so forth. Rather than depending entirely on the participants' possibly idiosyncratic, internalized normative information, we believe it is preferable to give the participants a common set of empirical, normative data including the difficulty of the test questions and the proportion of test takers who would be above or below each of the tentative cutscores that are being set. The information should be based on test takers who are representative of the people who will be taking the test when the cutscores are in operational use.

Participants in many cutscore studies are making difficult and unfamiliar judgments. They need all of the help that they can get to do a good job. The provision of normative information serves as a very useful reality check and can help the participants set reasonable cutscores.

The people who run cutscore studies differ on how much information should be provided to the participants and when it is best to provide it. We describe our opinion in section 3, *What You Have to Do Before You Set Cutscores.*

---

[4] In a criterion referenced test, the scores are compared to an absolute standard such as a cutscore. In a norm-referenced test, the scores are compared to the distribution of scores of some defined group.

3. WHAT YOU HAVE TO DO BEFORE YOU SET CUTSCORES

The activities involved in setting cutscores vary from one method of setting cutscores to another. There are, however, many important steps that must be completed before you set cutscores, regardless of the method you choose to set the cutscores. Those steps are described in this section of the manual.

3.1 Decide Whether or Not to Use Cutscores

We will refer to the person or group with the legal authority to decide whether or not to use cutscores as the *policymaker(s).* The first step in setting cutscores is for policymakers to decide that cutscores will be used. The approval of policymakers is needed at several steps in the process of setting cutscores, and the final, operational cutscores are set by policymakers.

Some uses of cutscores are mandated, as is the case with NCLB, and you may have no choice in the matter. But if you have the authority to decide whether or not to use cutscores, some questions to consider are these:

- What decisions will be made on the basis of the cutscores?
- Are there alternative methods of making those decisions?
- What harm could be caused by using cutscores?
- What harm would be caused by using the alternative methods?
- What are the benefits of using cutscores?
- What are the benefits of using the alternative methods?
- Do the benefits of using cutscores outweigh the harm?
- Are cutscores preferable to the alternative methods of making decisions?
- What is the overall objective of using cutscores?
- How will you know whether or not the objective has been met?

All that cutscores can do is place test takers into different categories on the basis of their test scores. Unless you plan to do something useful with that information, setting cutscores will not lead to beneficial consequences.

In short, if cutscores are optional, you should use them only if you have a good reason for setting cutscores, are reasonably confident that the use of cutscores will lead to the desired consequences, and have reason to believe that the positive consequences will outweigh the negative consequences.

3.2 Plan Ahead

Setting cutscores can be complicated, expensive and time-consuming. Lots of people may be required to serve as the participants who make the required judgments. People with specific skills (which we will describe) will be required to run the process. Planning is crucial to the success of the cutscore-setting process. Planning will help you to anticipate and avoid problems. (See section 7.1 for a list questions that will help you ensure the quality of your cutscore study as you plan and carry out the study.) We recommend that you create a written plan including a list of all the tasks that need to be completed, when they must be completed, and who will complete them. Your plan should also include a list of materials that you will need, and should specify who will provide each of the materials and when each of the materials must be provided.

> *We recommend that you create a written plan including a list of all the tasks that need to be completed, when they must be completed, and who will complete them.*

The remainder of this manual provides much of the information you will need to plan and carry out a cutscore study. We have provided a list of activities that should be included in your plan and a list of the materials you will need in section 8, *Tips.* If you are not comfortable planning and running complex projects, you should consider getting help from people who have experience in project management.

As part of your planning, find out the extent to which the policymakers who decided that cutscores should be set want to be involved in the process of setting cutscores. Do they wish to remain uninvolved? Do they wish to be kept informed of what you are doing? Do they wish to observe your work? Do they wish to be consulted on important decisions? Do they wish to be actively involved in your work? We recommend that you obtain the answers to the following questions concerning the policymakers.

- Who has to be involved in making decisions about the process of setting cutscores?

- Who has to approve the decisions?

- Who has to be informed about the decisions after they have been made?

We strongly suggest that early in your planning process you consult a lawyer who is familiar with testing issues, because tests used with cutscores have some special legal vulnerabilities in addition to the legal vulnerabilities faced by all tests.[5]

We think it is a good idea to keep the people who will be stakeholders in the cutscores informed about the major aspects of your plans. Cutscores are likely to be controversial. If they are a surprise to people, you are much more likely to have protests and legal challenges than if the people have had adequate prior notice.

Explain your reasons for using cutscores to the people likely to be affected, or (if they are children) to their parents or guardians. Tell them the steps you will follow, so it is clear that a careful process is in place. Give stakeholders a chance to comment on your plans. You may find, for instance, that stakeholders have misunderstood your plans and object to a use of the cutscores that you do not have in mind. For example, if you will not be using the cutscores to evaluate teachers, and teachers are concerned about that possibility, you will have an opportunity to alleviate their concerns. If you do plan to use the cutscores for a purpose that concerns stakeholders, you will have the opportunity to explain your decisions.

---

[5] After reviewing an earlier draft of this manual, our lawyer advised us not to offer any legal advice. We apologize for the lack of information on this important topic and urge you to consult a lawyer who can help you make your cutscores legally defensible.

3.3 Set Performance Levels and Performance Level Descriptors

What labels should you use for the categories into which you will place test takers? If you choose Basic, Proficient and Advanced, what does it mean to say that test takers are at each of the levels? What can people who are Proficient do that people who are Basic cannot do? If test takers pass a licensing test, what does it mean they know how to do? Questions like these are answered when you set performance levels and develop performance level descriptors.

3.3.1 Determine Performance Levels

Performance levels are the categories into which test takers will be classified on the basis of their test scores such as Pass and Fail, or Basic, Proficient, and Advanced. Usually, the performance levels that are used need to be set by or approved by the policymakers who are legally responsible for the decision to use cutscores. If policymakers do not decide on the performance levels to use, then you will have to do so.

If you have the option, consider the use of neutral labels, such as Level 1, Level 2, and Level 3, for performance levels. The neutral labels avoid the excess meanings that are often attached to more descriptive labels. If you do use numbers as labels for the performance levels, be sure to indicate which end of the scale represents the best performance. Make sure that people know whether Level 1 is the highest category or the lowest category.

> *Performance levels are the categories into which test takers will be classified on the basis of their test scores such as Pass and Fail, or Basic, Proficient, and Advanced.*

The purpose of the test should be considered in determining the number of performance levels needed. In many certification or licensure tests, only two levels are needed: Pass and Fail. NCLB requires states to develop at least three levels, one for Proficient, one level above Proficient and one below. Many states have added a fourth performance level, allowing them to differentiate between test takers who are close to Proficient (often called Basic) and those who are well below Proficient (often called Below Basic).

How many performance levels should you use? We believe that you should use the fewest performance levels that will meet your purpose for using cutscores. In our opinion you should probably use no more than four or five performance levels. It becomes increasingly difficult to describe and measure meaningful differences across levels as the number of levels increases. Also, the more performance levels you have, the more performance level descriptors and cutscores you will need to produce. The level of effort required to produce them can soon outpace available resources.

> *...use the fewest performance levels that will meet your purpose for using cutscores.*

3.3.2 Write Policy Definitions

After you determine the number and names of the levels, you need to develop a policy definition for each level except the lowest.[6] Policy definitions state the policymakers' position on "how good is good enough" at each defined performance level. For example, a score of Pass on a licensing test might be defined as, "having sufficient knowledge and skills to practice the occupation without danger to the public." In a K–12 educational context the policy definition for a performance level should be general enough to be applied to every grade and subject.

> *A good policy definition is concise, and provides clear distinctions across the levels.*

Generally, the very lowest level is implicitly defined as not meeting the requirements of the first explicitly defined level. For example, if Below Basic is the lowest level, it is implicitly defined as not meeting the requirements that have been explicitly specified for the Basic level.

A good policy definition is concise, and provides clear distinctions across the levels. The definition should be no more than a few sentences long. Because it is the basis of all further

---

[6] Some methods of setting cutscores based on matching questions to performance levels may be easier to apply if the lowest category is defined.

writing about the performance levels, you should carefully consider the wording. For example, the National Assessment of Educational Progress defines Basic, Proficient and Advanced as follows:[7]

> **Basic**: Partial mastery of prerequisite knowledge and skills that are fundamental for proficient work at each grade.
>
> **Proficient:** Solid academic performance for each grade assessed. Students reaching this level have demonstrated competency over challenging subject matter, including subject-matter knowledge, application of such knowledge to real-world situations, and analytical skills appropriate to the subject matter.
>
> **Advanced**: Superior performance.

3.3.3 Write Performance Level Descriptors

After the policy definitions have been completed, you should develop the performance level descriptors. The performance level descriptors state in words the knowledge and skills required to be in each defined level of performance for a specific assessment. You must develop the performance level descriptors before you set cutscores because the people who set the cutscores need the performance level descriptors to do their job effectively. In addition, the performance level descriptors are used to provide parents, educators, employers, the public, policymakers and other stakeholders with information on what people at each performance level know and are able to do, and what they need to know and be able to do to reach the next level. If performance level descriptors are vague and incomplete, the people who set the cutscores will have very poor targets and

> *The performance level descriptors state in words the knowledge and skills required to be in each defined level of performance for a specific assessment.*

---

[7] Below Basic remains undefined other than performance not yet at the Basic level.

will be more likely to disagree with one another than if the performance level descriptors are clear and complete.

We suggest that the performance level descriptors include some indications of the conditions under which the knowledge and skills are to be demonstrated. For example, to say that to pass a driver's license test, the applicant has to parallel park a car may seem clear, but some people who can parallel park on a quiet street may not be able to do so in heavy traffic. To say that a test taker who is Proficient in mathematics will be able to solve quadratic equations may seem clear, but some people who can solve quadratic equations if they are given the correct formula may not be able to do so in the absence of the formula, and so forth.

Each performance level descriptor covers a range of performance, just as a grade of B covers a range of performance from just slightly above C to just slightly below A. The people who set cutscores often have to focus on the *borderline* of a performance level to make the necessary distinctions between adjacent performance levels. The borderline separates a performance level from the one just below it. For example, the borderline of the grade of B would be the performance that distinguishes between the best grade C work and the poorest grade B work.

While it is possible for policymakers to write performance level descriptors, we do not recommend that practice. In an educational setting, performance level descriptors should be drafted by content experts and educators familiar with the curricular frameworks (content standards). They should also be familiar with what the test takers know and can do. In an occupational setting, the people who write the performance level descriptors should be licensed or certified practitioners of the occupation. They should be familiar with the knowledge and skills required by entry-level practitioners to protect the public from harm.

In a school setting, the resources needed to produce performance level descriptors across grades and subjects can be considerable because a separate performance level descriptor is needed for each defined performance level, in each subject, in each tested grade. For example, reading and math tests used to classify test takers as Below Basic, Basic, Proficient, or Advanced in grades 3–8 would require 36 separate performance level descriptors, if Below Basic is left undefined. If Below Basic is defined, then 48 separate performance level descriptors would be required.

The educators have to be recruited and trained to write performance level descriptors. In a large jurisdiction, you may have to pay for transportation, food, and lodging to bring the educators together for discussion. You may have to rent space for the meetings. You may have to compensate the educators or pay for their substitutes.

The test specifications can help shape the performance level descriptors. Take care, however, not to write the performance level descriptors that address a specific test question, because the same question is not likely to be included on all forms of the test. Focus on the knowledge and skills required to answer many similar questions, rather than on the particular aspects of a single test question.

The final product is often a paragraph detailing the knowledge and skills required to reach each performance level, although some descriptors are written in bulleted form. Here are some examples of performance level descriptors, the descriptors for fourth-grade math from the National Assessment of Educational Progress (NAEP):

> **Basic:** Fourth-graders performing at the Basic level should be able to estimate and use basic facts to perform simple computations with whole numbers; show some understanding of fractions and decimals; and solve some simple real-world problems in all NAEP content areas (Number Properties and Operations, Measurement, Geometry, Data Analysis and Probability, Algebra). Students at this level should be able to use—though not always accurately—four-function calculators, rulers, and geometric shapes. Their written responses will often be minimal and presented without supporting information.

> **Proficient:** Fourth-graders performing at the Proficient level should be able to use whole numbers to estimate, compute, and determine whether results are reasonable. They should have a conceptual understanding of fractions and decimals; be able to solve real-world problems in all NAEP content areas; and use four-function calculators, rulers, and geometric shapes appropriately. Students

performing at the Proficient level should employ problem-solving strategies such as identifying and using appropriate information. Their written solutions should be organized and presented both with supporting information and explanations of how they were achieved.

Advanced: Fourth-graders performing at the Advanced level should be able to solve complex and nonroutine real-world problems in all NAEP content areas. They should display mastery in the use of four-function calculators, rulers, and geometric shapes. The students are expected to draw logical conclusions and justify answers and solution processes by explaining why, as well as how, they were achieved. They should go beyond the obvious in their interpretations and be able to communicate their thoughts clearly and concisely.

When several grades are involved (as required by NCLB and other state accountability systems), the performance level descriptors should be aligned across grades. For example, the performance level descriptor for Proficient performance in reading in grade 5 should require more knowledge and skills than are required to be Proficient in grade 4, but less than are required to be Proficient in grade 6. If you do not pay attention to alignment across grades, anomalies are likely.

> *When several grades are involved, the performance level descriptors should be aligned across grades.*

Holding simultaneous, independent meetings to write performance level descriptors for all grades 3–8 is not likely to result in aligned performance level descriptors. A more effective practice is to share the descriptors written for one grade level with the people writing descriptors for adjacent grade levels. You will have to review the results for consistency and alignment across grades. If inconsistencies are found, you will need a mechanism for obtaining consensus on the revisions, which may involve additional meetings of educators.

If there are only a few performance level descriptors (such as Pass and Fail for a licensing test) it is possible to write the performance level descriptors and then set cutscores at the same meeting, assuming sufficient time is available. If you need more than two or three performance level descriptors, however, we recommend that you complete the performance level descriptors before you hold the meetings to set the cutscores. The final step in writing performance level descriptors should be a formal approval process by the appropriate policymakers.

We recommend that you write the performance level descriptors before test development begins, if it is possible to do so.

> **...write the performance level descriptors before test development begins, if it is possible to do so.**

If the performance level descriptors are available in time, they can serve as a guide for the content to be measured by the test and as a guide for the intended difficulty of the questions. For example, if test developers know how Basic, Proficient and Advanced are defined, they can ensure that the test has sufficient questions to measure the knowledge and skills included in the performance level descriptors for those levels, and the test can be designed to classify test takers reliably.

3.4 Decide If You Should Use a Cutscore Based on the Total Score or on Subscores

If the test yields two or more scores based on parts of the test (usually called subscores), you will have to decide whether to have a single cutscore for the total score on the test, or separate cutscores for each subscore. If there is a single cutscore for the test, higher scores on some parts of the test can compensate for lower scores on other parts of the test. (Therefore, total score cutscores are often called *compensatory* cutscores.) If there is a separate cutscore applied to each subscore, scoring high on one subscore does not compensate for a low score on a different subscore. (Such cutscores are often called *conjunctive* cutscores.) Similarly, if a decision rule uses information from two or more tests, you can apply a single cutscore to a combined score for all the tests or apply a separate cutscore to the score on each test.

For example, a literature test may have separate subscores for American literature and English literature. A total score cutscore is appropriate if you do not care how the test taker's competence is distributed across those two areas, as long as the test taker knows a certain amount about literature. Separate cutscores for each subscore are appropriate if a certain amount of knowledge about English literature is required of all test takers, no matter how much they know about American literature, and vice versa.

The reliability of the subscores is an important consideration in deciding whether or not to use separate cutscores for each subscore. Because subscores are based on only a subset of the questions in a test, each subscore is necessarily less reliable than is the total score on the test. One or more of the subscores may be quite unreliable. A test taker's score may be heavily influenced by the luck of the draw, with respect to the specific questions or tasks included (and, for constructed-response tests, the specific people who score that test taker's responses). Total test cutscores reduce the effects of these chance factors. Applying a separate cutscore to each subscore makes the classifications of the test takers depend heavily on the least reliable subscore. Therefore, we recommend that you use a single total score cutscore unless it does not make sense to do so.

> *...we recommend that you use a single total score cutscore unless it does not make sense to do so.*

There are situations in which a single cutscore does not make sense and separate cutscores are necessary. One example is the battery of tests required for a driver's license. Outstandingly good driving skill does not compensate for poor vision or for a lack of knowledge of the rules of the road. Excellent vision or exceptionally thorough knowledge of the laws does not compensate for a lack of ability to control the car.

It is possible to combine total score cutscores and subscore cutscores in a single decision rule. For example, if a test of teaching skills has separate scores for classroom management (50 points), and management of instruction (50 points), a decision rule could require at least 30 points on each subscore and a total score of at least 70.

3.5 Select a Method for Conducting the Cutscore Study

You will have to decide which method(s) to use to conduct your cutscore study. We will offer advice for choosing a method in section 5. As we have stressed, all methods of setting cutscores depend on judgments. Cutscore studies can be divided into four broad classes depending on the kinds of judgments that the participants make. In one large class of cutscore studies, participants make judgments about test questions. In a smaller class of cutscore studies, participants make judgments about patterns of subscores, often called profiles. In another large class of cutscore studies, participants make judgments about individual people or the products made by those people.[8] In the fourth class of cutscore studies, participants make judgments about groups of people, rather than about individuals. There are also a few compromise methods that combine absolute and normative judgments.

3.5.1 Judgments of Test Questions

The methods based on judgments of test questions are relatively convenient. It is almost always possible to obtain judgments about test questions. Some of the methods can be applied either before or after the test is administered. In fact, for several methods the judgments can be made on a pool of questions even before the questions to be included in a test form have been selected from the pool. The process of making judgments about test questions focuses the participants' attention closely on the content of the test questions. Another advantage is that many participants can be included, which is helpful in large jurisdictions or in situations, such as high school exit examinations, in which wide participation is politically necessary.

> **The methods based on judgments of test questions are relatively convenient. It is almost always possible to obtain judgments about test questions.**

However, in most methods based on judgments of test questions, the type of judgment called for is unfamiliar and may be difficult for participants. The participants are asked to decide how a test taker whose performance falls on the borderline of a

---

[8] Some authors have separated methods based on judgments of people from methods based on judgments of products. We believe the similarities far outweigh the differences and have treated methods based on those judgments together.

performance level would be likely to respond to each of the questions on the test. Because of the hypothetical nature of these judgments, we believe that these methods need a "reality check." If you use one of the methods, you should supplement it with information about the actual test performance of real test takers, if you possibly can. If the additional information clearly indicates that the results of the method do not describe the performance of a borderline test taker, you should be prepared to admit that the method may not have worked well and to choose the cutscore in some other way.

Because of their convenience, cutscores based on judgments of test questions are much more widely used than cutscores based on judgments of people or products. You should be aware that some psychometricians have attacked methods of setting cutscores based on judgments of test questions as "fundamentally flawed" because of the cognitive difficulty of making the required judgments. Other psychometricians, however, have defended these methods, and they remain the most popular means of setting cutscores. In our experience, participants in cutscore studies seem able to make the necessary judgments. We have never had a participant withdraw from a cutscore study because he or she felt that the judgments were impossible to make. The participants do, however, need training and practice before they can make the judgments required by many methods of setting cutscores.

3.5.2 Judgments of Profiles of Scores

Some tests are made of several parts, each with a separate subscore. The set of all of the subscores for a test taker is called a *profile* of scores. For example, a language test may have separate subscores for reading, writing, listening, and speaking. Consider two profiles of scores on that test: (10, 0, 10, 0) and (6, 5, 4, 5). Both profiles have a total score of 20, but the subscores on the two profiles are very different. The participants in a cutscore study may believe that writing and speaking are essential parts of language ability. If they do, they may find the first profile unacceptable and the second profile acceptable. The main advantage of methods based on judgments about profiles of scores is that they can take account of information contained in the subscores, beyond the information that is conveyed by the total score.

3.5.3 Judgments of People or Products

The methods based on judgments of people or products require two types of information about each test taker: (1) the person's test score, and (2) a judgment of the level of the test taker's knowledge and skills. The judgment about the test taker's knowledge and skills may be based on knowledge of the test taker's typical performance, observation of the test taker's performance (on the test or in a special situation arranged especially for the cutscore study), or an evaluation of some product made by the test taker, such as an essay or an architectural drawing.

The main advantage of these methods is that they are based on real people or real things rather than on judgments about how a hypothetical group of test takers might perform. People in our society are accustomed to judging other people's skills, behaviors or products as adequate or inadequate for some purpose— especially in educational and occupational settings. Teachers judge their students, supervisors judge the workers they supervise, and professionals judge their colleagues. Therefore, making this type of judgment is likely to be a familiar task.

3.5.4 Judgments of Groups of People

The methods based on judgments about groups of people require judgments about the levels of knowledge and skills that exist in some defined group or groups of people. The methods are most easily applied when the required judgments are routinely made. In occupational settings, for example, supervisors may evaluate employees on relevant factors. The main advantage of these methods is that the judgments are grounded in reality.

3.5.5 Our Preference

We believe that methods based on judgments about real people or about real products are preferable to other classes of methods, and we recommend their use if you can obtain the necessary data. There are two main reasons why we prefer those methods. Making judgments about real people or products such as work samples is likely to be a familiar task to participants because such judgments are often made by educators about students or by supervisors about employees. Furthermore, the judgments are anchored in reality. The methods based on judgments of test questions, however, require participants to make judgments about how a hypothetical group of test takers would respond to test questions. Such judgments are likely to be unfamiliar to participants.

If you use a method based on judgments of test questions we strongly recommend that you augment your study with data on the performance of real test takers. We will provide more information on the advantages and disadvantages of specific methods in section 4, *Overviews of Methods of Setting Cutscores*.

> **If you use a method based on judgments of test questions we strongly recommend that you augment your study with data on the performance of real test takers.**

3.6 Decide How to Conduct the Study

There are decisions you must make about exactly how to implement your cutscore study once you have chosen a method. These decisions include the number of judgments you want your participants to make, the data you want to provide to the participants, and how you will combine their judgments to calculate a cutscore.

All cutscores depend on judgment. We believe that participants can make better judgments if they are given information about question difficulty, the judgments of their colleagues, and the percent of test takers that would be in each performance level if the cutscores based on the participants' judgments at various stages of the procedure had been applied.

It has become a common practice to have several rounds of judgments and to provide feedback on the judgments and normative information about the test questions between the rounds. Some of the newer methods we describe include several iterations of judgments and the provision of normative information to the participants between iterations as inherent aspects of the method. The older methods do not specify the number of iterations to conduct, nor do they specify the type of information to provide to the participants between iterations. We believe, however, that you should use two or three iterations of judgments and give normative information to participants between iterations.

Studies using the same method can differ by design in the amount of discussion among participants, the number of times participants make their judgments and whether or not data are given to participants. If data are given to participants, studies can differ in the types of data given to participants, and when the data are given to participants. Each of these possible variations will require a decision about the way you run your cutscore study.

3.6.1 Discussion among Participants

You need to decide what the participants will discuss with each other and how much time they should spend on each topic. Some topics are required by the method that you choose. For example, many methods require discussion of the knowledge and skills of test takers at the borderline of each defined performance level. For methods based on judgments about test questions in K–12 educational contexts, the participants should discuss the relevant content standards or curriculum frameworks, the test blueprints, and what students have to know and be able to do to answer each question correctly.

Decide whether participants should be given the opportunity to discuss their operational ratings with one another and then be given a chance to amend their ratings. Because participants are selected to represent different points of view, they will probably have different opinions about cutscores. If you allow the participants to share these perspectives in group discussion, you will increase the chances that their cutscores will tend to converge. A common practice is to have participants make independent judgments without any discussion in the first round of judgments. The participants then are given an opportunity to see all of their ratings and to discuss their differences. The participants discuss with one another why they made the ratings they did and what considerations they used. Encourage the participants to listen to their colleagues with an open mind. The participants should not succumb to peer pressure, but they should consider what their colleagues have said when they make their next round of judgments.

Another decision you need to make about participant discussion is how to seat the participants for their discussions with each other. The seating arrangement will affect the way the participants interact. If you have, for example, 20 participants, different conversations will occur if you seat all 20 participants around one conference table than if you split them into 4 smaller tables with 5 participants around each table. There are pros and cons to each configuration. Using the larger table gives each participant the opportunity to hear what every other participant says, but fewer participants may have an opportunity to speak. Furthermore, some participants may not be comfortable speaking in a larger group. The smaller tables encourage greater participation from each individual participant but tend to limit the range of opinions heard by any one participant. An additional advantage to the use of separate tables is that it allows you to see the cutscores produced by different groups of participants, if you complete one or two rounds of judgments without discussion between the tables. The data from the different groups will allow you to estimate how much the cutscore changes when different groups of participants are used.

If you use the smaller tables, we recommend that you have some whole room discussions in addition to the table discussions. Ask a representative from each table to summarize the discussions at his or her table so that all of the participants can join the discussion. Consistent with time constraints, allow all of the participants who want to take part in the whole room discussion an opportunity to do so.

3.6.2 Data on Questions

Another variation in cutscore studies is the degree to which data about the test questions are provided to the participants. For example, you must decide whether you want the participants to know what percent of test takers answered each multiple-choice question correctly or what the average score on each constructed-response question was. Some facilitators believe that it is important to give the participants as much information as is available to help inform their decisions. Other facilitators, however, are concerned that too much normative data can confuse the participants or overly influence their judgments.

Some facilitators prefer to provide information on question difficulty for all of the questions. Other facilitators prefer to provide data only on certain questions such as those questions that participants disagreed about. There is no single correct method of providing the information, but we believe it is certainly better to provide some information rather than none at all. If you do provide data on question difficulty, it is important to tell the participants what group of test takers the difficulty statistics refer to. It is best if the group is representative of the test takers who will be taking the operational test. If that is not the case, the participants need to know how the group differs from those test takers.

If you decide to provide data on questions, the next decision is when to provide it. Should it be provided before the first judgment is made? After the first round of judgments? Just before the final round? Some of these decisions are dependent on the methodology. For example, in the Bookmark method, the questions are ordered by difficulty, so even if the participants do not know the percent of students who answer each question correctly, they do know the relative difficulty of the questions before they make their first judgment. Facilitators often provide question-level data after the first round of judgments in a cutscore study, but sometimes they give this information before the first round of judgments.

In addition to data on questions, it may be helpful to provide participants with data on the distribution of test scores. Again, the data should be based on test takers representative of those who will take the operational test. Typically, facilitators do not give this information until after the participants have made an initial round of judgments based on the content of the test or the responses to the test. Often this information is withheld until just before the last round of judgments.

3.6.3 Impact Data

You also need to decide whether to show participants the effect of their cutscores on the percent of test takers in each performance level. Often called "impact data" or "consequences data," this information gives participants an idea of how their current recommendations would cause test takers to be distributed across performance levels (e.g., the percent that would be classified as Basic, the percent that would be classified as Proficient, and the percent that would be classified as Advanced).

If you decide to use impact data, you will also have to decide when to provide the data, and how much detail to provide. Your decision will depend on whether you believe the data will help the participants make better decisions or will contaminate their judgments of what test takers should know and be able to do to reach a performance level.

We believe that impact data based on test takers representative of those who will take the operational test can help participants to set more appropriate cutscores. We recommend providing such data to the participants. In K–12 educational testing it has become common practice to provide impact data because the percent of students reaching Proficient or higher has important consequences under the *No Child Left Behind* legislation. Participants find it helpful to consider such data. Similarly, participants setting a cutscore for a high school graduation test and participants setting a passing score on a certification test find it helpful to consider the percent of test takers who would pass, to evaluate the reasonableness of their cutscore. Figure 1 shows a useful way of displaying the data.

Figure 1. Test Score Distribution, Cutscores, and Percent of Students Classified into Each Performance Level

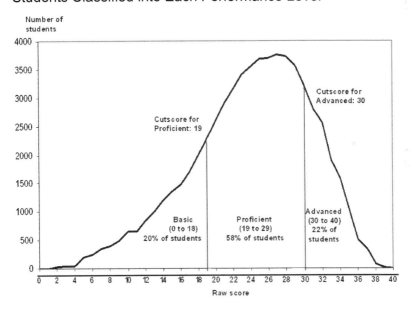

If you decide that impact data should be provided, you then need to determine when to provide these data to the participants. The timing should depend on the weight you want the participants to give to the data. The later in the process you provide the data, the less influence it will have on the cutscore. To reduce the influence of the impact data and to maintain the focus on absolute judgments, introduce the data late in the process such as just before the last round of judgments. If you want the data to have a greater influence on the outcome, then introduce the data earlier in the process, such as immediately after the first round of judgments. Typically, in K–12 cutscore studies, the impact data are given after the participants have had one or two opportunities to make independent judgments, just before they make their final judgment.

Sometimes, the impact data should be given great weight. Consider, for example, a situation in which cutscores have already been set for grades 3, 4, 6, and 7. The only cutscore remaining to be set is at grade 5. If the percentages of students scoring at or above the cutscore are approximately the same across grades 3, 4, 6, and 7, you may want to tell the participants early in the cutscore study where they would need to place the cutscore in grade 5 to have a similar percentage of students reaching it. (See section 9, *Consistency Across Grades,* for more discussion of such situations.)

If you provide the impact data, we suggest that you give the participants an opportunity to discuss their reactions to the data, including how the actual data compare to their expectations. In our experience, participants request guidance about whether it is acceptable to change their earlier judgments substantially in light of the impact data, or whether they should make only small adjustments. Opinions differ. Our opinion is that if the participants believe that the impact data indicate that their interim cutscores are inappropriate, they should be allowed to adjust the cutscores as much as they desire. They should, however, keep the test content and the meanings of the performance levels in mind as they make the adjustments. If the participants who set the cutscores think that the cutscores are unreasonable and are unwilling to stand behind them, it will be difficult to convince anybody else that the cutscores are appropriate.

Finally, if you have made the decision to use impact data, you need to consider how much data to give to the participants. In addition to showing the results for the entire population of test takers, you may show the impact data separately for different subpopulations, such as for gender, racial, and ethnic groups. In K–12 educational settings, it may be useful to break out the data further for groups defined by such factors as poverty status, use of English as a second language, migrant status, and disability status because separate reporting for those groups as well as for the gender, racial, and ethnic groups is typically required for accountability purposes.

You will need to decide, in advance of the meeting, at which point additional data are likely to become overwhelming and confusing rather than helpful. Keep in mind that most participants are not used to working with lots of data and may find it difficult to attend to data on several groups at once.

Also, data based on subpopulations can be difficult to interpret if the number of students in a particular demographic group is very small. The smaller the group of students, the more the performance of a few students will affect the results obtained for the group. For example, consider a group of 30 students in which three students generally perform at a level that is just barely Proficient. It may happen that on the day of the test one of the three students is not feeling well, another is tired, and a third one has bad luck in guessing on a few questions. In this hypothetical but realistic example, the percent of the group classified as Proficient will drop by 10 percentage points because three students performed less well than they usually do. Our point is that chance may play a large role in determining the impact of cutscores on a small group. Therefore, you should ask the statistician working with you to help decide when a group becomes too small to provide reliable impact data.

3.6.4 Number of Iterations

You will need to specify the number of iterations or rounds of judgments in your cutscore study. Some cutscore studies use only one round of judgments, and we have heard of studies that used as many as five rounds of judgments. We have found little change in cutscores after three rounds so we do not suggest using more than three rounds unless you have a specific reason to do so. If you want to give the participants an opportunity to discuss their differences before making their final judgments, then you will need to have a minimum of two rounds. You may decide to include one additional round to give impact data separately from the information about other participants' judgments. If you decide to provide other types of information, such as how cutscores are aligned across grades in an educational setting, you can either include additional rounds or provide that information at the time you provide one or more other types of information.

How many rounds of judgments should you conduct? Even if our description of a cutscore method does not specify that iterations should take place, we suggest that you have at least two rounds of judgments and that you consider having three rounds. We further suggest that the initial round of judgments be done in the absence of any normative information. Between the first and second rounds of judgments, provide information about question difficulty (if that has not been done previously) and reveal the judgments and cutscores generated by the participants in the first round. If you have a third round of judgments, we suggest waiting to reveal the percentages of test takers who would fall into the various performance levels until after the second round. (Use the cutscores that resulted from the second round.) If you do not have a third round, we suggest using the cutscores that resulted from the first round to compute the percentages of test takers who would fall into the various performance levels and giving the participants this information before the second (final) round.

3.6.5 Combining Information across Participants

Many of the methods that we describe result in a separate cutscore from each participant. How should you combine these individual cutscores? One way is simply to average the scores in the usual way (add them up and divide by the number of participants). This type of average is called the *mean*. The disadvantage of using the mean is that it allows one participant with a very high or very low cutscore to have a disproportionately large influence on the result.

A second way to combine the scores is to take the *median*. To find the median, first list the participants' cutscores in order from highest to lowest. (If a cutscore appears more than once, be sure to list it as many times as it appears.) If the number of participants is an odd number, the median is simply the middle cutscore. If the number of participants is even, the median is halfway between the two middle cutscores. The advantage of using the median is that extremely high or extremely low cutscores do not have a great influence on the result. The disadvantage of using the median is that it disregards a great deal of information by focusing entirely on the middle cutscore.

A third way to combine the scores represents a compromise between the mean and the median. It is called the *trimmed mean*. To compute the trimmed mean, simply eliminate the highest and lowest cutscores and average the remaining cutscores in the usual way. (You have seen this process in use if you have watched the Olympic competitions in figure skating.)

Depending on the number of participants, you may choose to eliminate the highest two cutscores and the lowest two cutscores, or the highest and lowest three cutscores, or more. How much trimming to do is up to you and your statistician, but be aware of the possible negative consequences if participants believe you are "throwing out" too much of their work. See Figure 2 for examples of the computation of the mean, median, and trimmed mean.

Figure 2. Example of Calculation of Mean, Median and Trimmed Mean

Participant	Participant's Cutscore
A	92.50
B	77.25
C	67.00
D	66.67
E	65.33

Mean = (92.50 + 77.25 + 67.00 + 66.67 + 65.33) / 5 = 73.75
Trimmed mean = (77.25 + 67.00 + 66.67) / 3 = 70.31
Median = Middle Cutscore = 67.00

You should decide which way you will combine the cutscores before the start of the cutscore meeting. If you are going to use the trimmed mean for averaging the scores, you should let the participants know this fact, and how much trimming you will do, *before* you calculate the cutscore from their judgments. Otherwise, the participants who are "trimmed" may suspect that you are discriminating against them.

It can be risky to use the simple mean because it is open to the influence of the most extreme participants. In our experience, it is often the case that the participants who set cutscores that are *far* higher or *far* lower than those of their colleagues have either failed to understand the task, or have come to the meeting with predetermined beliefs about what the cutscore should be. For example, we have encountered participants who believed

40

> **The trimmed mean is a good compromise between wasting data and avoiding the influence of extreme participants.**

that tests are harmful and who therefore intended to set the cutscore so low that nobody would fail. Therefore, we prefer the median or the trimmed mean to the mean. The trimmed mean is a good compromise between wasting data and avoiding the influence of extreme participants.

The average you obtain is not likely to be a whole number. You may, for example, obtain an average of 18.36 for the Proficient cutscore. In that case, what should the cutscore be? In one view, it is appropriate to follow mathematical convention and round to the nearest whole number, making the cutscore 18. In another view, the result of the cutscore study showed that the test taker has to score over 18 to be considered Proficient, making the cutscore 19.

Which view should you adopt? We think that the answer depends on which type of misclassification is considered more harmful in your particular situation. If it is more harmful to pass a test taker who should fail than it is to fail a test taker who should pass, then 19 is more appropriate than 18. If it is more harmful to fail a test taker who should pass than to pass a test taker who should fail, then 18 is more appropriate than 19. We recommend that you decide, before the cutscore meeting begins, how you will handle averages that are not integers. We think that you should base the decision on judgments about which type of misclassification is considered worse.

3.6.6 Would or Should?

For the methods based on judgments of test questions, there has been some controversy about whether it is better to ask participants to make judgments about how borderline test takers *should* perform on test questions or on how borderline test takers *would* perform on test questions. We have found that participants who focus on how test takers *should* perform usually expect much more from test takers within a performance level than do participants who focus on how test takers *would* perform. For example, when we ask participants to describe how a group of borderline Proficient test takers *should* perform on a question, we hear responses such as, "Well, they <u>all</u> *should* be able to get the question right, but I'd bet that only about 80 percent actually *would* get it right." Because *would* generally implies reality to participants and *should* generally implies an ideal state, we recommend using *would* rather than *should* when you ask participants about the performance of borderline test takers.

3.7 Obtain Staff and Facilities for the Cutscore Meeting

Although staff and facilities may seem like simple administrative considerations, they have large implications for the success of a cutscore study and should be given careful attention.

3.7.1 Staff

There are five roles to fill when staffing a cutscore meeting: facilitator, subject-matter expert, test expert, statistician (or psychometrician), and document manager. A person can fill more than one role. For example, the facilitator can also be a subject-matter expert or the test expert can also be a statistician. We recommend, however, that you have at least three people staff a cutscore meeting: one who can fill the

There are five roles to fill when staffing a cutscore meeting: facilitator, subject-matter expert, test expert, statistician (or psychometrician), and document manager.

role of the facilitator, one who can fill the role of the statistician, and one who can fill the role of the document manager. Any person trying to fill two of those roles at one meeting is likely to be required to do two different tasks at the same time.

The facilitator takes overall responsibility for the outcomes of the meeting at which cutscores are set. He or she runs the meeting, trains the participants (and staff as necessary), and coordinates the work of the other staff members. The facilitator has to know about setting cutscores in general and should be extremely comfortable with the method in use. He or she should be experienced in running meetings and in training adults. The facilitator ensures that all of the steps are carried out in the appropriate sequence and in the allotted time. He or she should be able to determine priorities and handle problems. (See section 8, *Tips,* for a discussion of the kinds of problems to expect.)

The facilitator should have no vested interest in the outcomes of the cutscore meeting. A facilitator who has a reason to want the cutscore to be in a certain part of the score range may affect the outcomes of the cutscore meeting accordingly, even if he or she tries to be impartial. Even if the facilitator succeeds in being impartial, the use of a facilitator with a vested interest in the value of the cutscore may lower public confidence in the results. Similarly, it is best if the facilitator does not feel a need to defend the test questions from criticism.

> *The facilitator should have no vested interest in the outcomes of the cutscore meeting.*

Some jurisdictions run two or more cutscore meetings at the same time. It is fairly common to have cutscore meetings for tests in different subject areas run simultaneously. For example, reading and math participants may gather together for the general aspects of training and then separate to work on definitions of borderline performance and to set the cutscores for their respective subjects. Within a subject, participants setting cutscores in adjacent grades may meet separately to set cutscores for their grades and join together after important segments of their work have been completed to help ensure that the cutscores are appropriately aligned across the grades. If the resources are available to do so, it can be very useful to run two parallel cutscore meetings for the same test. Doing so allows you to check the results of the two sets of participants for consistency. If the results of the two groups differ, you can bring the groups together to resolve their differences. Jurisdictions with simultaneous meetings usually have an overall facilitator in addition to a facilitator for each separate group.

In the following descriptions of the methods, we will assume that you are the facilitator. Ideally, you should be trained in a cutscore method by an experienced facilitator, should watch an experienced facilitator use the method, and then should use the method under the guidance of an experienced facilitator, before you use the method on your own. If that is not possible, we very strongly recommend that you at least have a rehearsal with people similar to the participants before you run an operational cutscore meeting for the first time.

The subject-matter expert responds to any content or curricular issues raised by the participants. For example, in a K–12 educational testing context, a question may be raised about whether the teaching of division in a particular grade includes division of a fraction by a fraction. In an occupational context, a question may be raised about whether or not a particular competency is required of entry-level employees. Even if the participants are themselves subject-matter experts, it is helpful to have a person available who can give the "official" response.

At almost every cutscore setting session we have attended, participants criticized some of the test questions for being too hard or too easy, for being irrelevant, for being confusing, for being tricky, for having no correct answer or for having more than one correct answer, for being generally unfair, or for being offensive, racist, or sexist. Questions about test development, testing policy and the effects of using the test are also common. Questions we have heard include, "Why is the test being given? What happens to people who fail? Can people who fail take the test over? What accommodations are made for people with disabilities? The test is too hard (easy). Who decided how hard (easy) the test should be? How many of the test developers are African American? What was done to ensure the fairness of the test?" A testing expert who is familiar with the test under consideration should be available to answer questions. If it is possible, arrange for a policymaker to be present or available by speaker phone to answer questions about testing policy.

The role of the statistician varies with the method used to set the cutscore. For some methods, the statistician's task is limited to calculating averages and percentages. For other methods, however, the statistician is called on to use Item Response Theory or logistic regression. In many cases, the statistician must work rapidly while the participants wait for the results. It is highly useful to have the statistician pre-program automated spreadsheets to make the necessary calculations. Some large cutscore meetings have used portable scanners to enter the data provided by the participants into the spreadsheets. You should require an independent check of the data entry for accuracy, particularly if manual data entry is used.

The role of the document manager also varies with the method employed to set the cutscore. Even the simplest method requires keeping track of lots of papers such as test booklets, participants' rating forms, non-disclosure forms, travel vouchers, and so forth. The document manager's tasks are to ensure that all necessary documents are available when they are needed, given to the participants at the appropriate time, collected from all participants when the documents have been completed, checked for accuracy as necessary, and safely maintained until no longer needed. Keeping track of all confidential materials during the cutscore study is a large responsibility. Methods that use lots of paperwork and have many participants may require more than one document manager to keep the meeting running smoothly. The document manager may also play a role in entering data or in checking the accuracy of the data entry.

3.7.2 Facilities

You will need a meeting room with adequate space for each participant to sit at a table with space for a test book, a sheet of instructions, and various other documents depending on the method. Some methods require a number of small tables with a group of participants at each table. For some tests you will need facilities for participants to play audio or video recordings of test takers' responses to performance questions. Each participant should have a good view of a screen, flip chart, or white board in front of the room. If the room is very large or noisy, a public address system may be necessary. Participants will spend a lot of time reading, so adequate lighting is required. The work space and nearby restrooms should be accessible for people with disabilities. If you are working with confidential materials, you will need a lockable storage space and a way to secure the meeting room during meals, breaks and overnight.

The document manager will need a secure place to keep confidential materials and space to store other papers. The statistician will need a table with room for a computer and space for data entry. The facilitator will need a laptop computer, projector and screen, large flip charts or a white board, and markers.

A cutscore meeting is likely to take two or three days. In large jurisdictions, participants will need lodging near the meeting room. If participants have to leave the building for lunch and coffee breaks, it is difficult to keep everybody on schedule, so you should provide meals and coffee breaks for the participants, if possible.

Internet "meetings," sometimes called "Web conferencing," can be used to set cutscores. There are several commercial sites on the Internet that allow participants to interact as though they were at a meeting. Internet meetings result in very significant savings because there are no costs for transportation, food, lodging, or meeting rooms. Each participant requires a telephone for discussions with other participants and the facilitator, a computer, and an Internet connection to a Web site for viewing documents and entering responses. You will need a scanner if you have to input documents that are not available as electronic files. Internet meetings have been shown to work reasonably well for setting cutscores, but we admit a preference for live meetings. We find it much easier to judge whether or not participants understand our presentations and follow our instructions when we are in the same room with them than when we are on the Internet. It is also easier to make sure participants are attending to the right documents and to control confidential materials in a live meeting than on the Internet.

3.8 Select Participants

Two sets of participants are likely to set different cutscores, even when using the same procedures and working with the same facilitator. Therefore, an important task in any cutscore study is choosing participants who are qualified to make the necessary judgments and who are representative of all qualified participants. You should set specifications for the characteristics of the group of participants and obtain approval of the specifications

...an important task in any cutscore study is choosing participants who are qualified to make the necessary judgments and who are representative of all qualified participants.

from the policymakers who commissioned the cutscores. If you are careful in selecting qualified and representative participants to meet an approved set of specifications, you will be in a better position to defend the cutscore selected at the meeting.

3.8.1 Who Should Participate?

Cutscores are based on judgments. Whose judgments should you use? The answer varies somewhat with the method you choose to apply, and we will discuss those differences when we describe the various methods. There are some general rules, however, that apply regardless of method. First and most important, the participants must be qualified to decide what level of the knowledge and skills measured by the test is necessary to meet the purpose for setting the cutscore. For example, if a test of occupational knowledge is being used as a requirement for a nuclear power plant operator's license, the participants must be able to decide how much knowledge about operating the power plant is necessary to protect the public. The participants should be licensed operators of nuclear power plants and be able to distinguish the "must know" aspects of the task from the "nice to know" aspects. It is common to set criteria for years of relevant experience among participants. For certification tests, it is common to require that participants have some experience in supervising entry-level employees.

It is also important that the selected participants be representative of all the qualified people who could be participants with respect to attributes that are relevant to the test. If practices differ in different jurisdictions, the participants should represent the relevant jurisdictions. If some qualified people have been trained on the job and some have been trained in formal training programs, the participants should include people with both types of training. If qualified people work in different types of institutions, and if the jobs differ, the participants should include people from the different types of institutions, and so forth. In educational accountability settings, for example, the selected participants should represent the different types of schools in the jurisdiction. Also in educational settings, teachers of different types of students who will take the test should be represented. For example, teachers of students with disabilities, and teachers of gifted students should be included among the participants. In general, all important points of view should be represented among the participants.

In addition, the participants should be representative of all qualified people with respect to demographic characteristics. For example, if about half of the people qualified to be participants are women, then about half of the participants you select should be women. If about 15 percent of the people qualified to be participants are African American, then about 15 percent of the participants you select should be African American, and so forth.

3.8.2 Levels of Controversy

For the task of selecting participants, we have found it useful to distinguish among expected levels of controversy in the setting and use of the cutscore. The least controversial use of cutscores is likely to be in highly technical areas, such as licensing or certification tests for nuclear power plant operators, arthroscopic surgeons, air traffic controllers, and so forth. The pool of qualified participants will be relatively small and easy to identify through professional organizations or licensing bureaus. The participants must themselves hold the licenses or certificates for which passing the test is a requirement and are likely to be in fairly close agreement about what constitutes acceptable practice. In these cases, there is likely to be little public interest in the process as the cutscores are being set and few arguments among members of the general public about the test or the cutscore. Of course, the participants should be representative of different types of practice within the occupation and should represent the demographic diversity of members of the occupation.

The next higher level of controversy is likely to occur with academic tests used for accountability systems, such as those required by NCLB. The pool of qualified participants is larger, there is likely to be less agreement among them, and there is more public interest in the process and its outcomes. For educational accountability tests, the participants should consist mostly of teachers, with possibly some school administrators and curriculum specialists. The teachers should be very familiar with the characteristics of test takers in the tested grades, with the state content standards, and with the curricular materials that are in use. Take care to represent different types of schools and different types of localities in the appropriate proportions. For example, unreasonably high cutscores might be set if teachers from schools in wealthy suburbs were greatly over-represented. The demographic diversity of all educators in the jurisdiction in which the cutscores will be used (such as a state) should be represented among the participants.

The most controversial situations are those in which there is a great deal of public interest and in which many different types of people are qualified to be participants. In such cases, a great deal of disagreement about the appropriate cutscore is likely. For example, if a reading test is being used as a requirement for high school graduation, the participants must be qualified to decide what a high school diploma should indicate about a person's reading ability. A lot of people are qualified to have opinions on that topic and the opinions differ greatly. Some people think a high school diploma should indicate readiness for college level work. Others think a high school diploma should

48

indicate minimal mastery of basic skills. The many qualified participants would include not only high school teachers, but also college admissions officers, military recruiters, human resource professionals, employers of high school graduates, union representatives, community college professors, parents, educational administrators, policymakers, and so forth. Demographic representation is particularly important for the panel of participants in a cutscore study for a controversial test.

> When you select the participants for the cutscore study, you are really deciding whose standards of proficiency will be incorporated into the cutscore.

When you select the participants for the cutscore study, you are really deciding whose standards of proficiency will be incorporated into the cutscore. Your selection of participants can greatly affect the cutscore. Deciding which groups the participants should represent, and deciding how many members of each group should be selected are policy issues rather than measurement issues. Therefore, we believe it is important to specify the desired characteristics of the total group of participants before you begin selecting individual participants.

We suggest that you have your specifications for the total group of participants reviewed and approved by the relevant policymakers. Then start recruiting participants to meet the specifications that the policymakers have approved. After the invited participants have had a chance to respond to the invitation, check the characteristics of the resulting set of participants against your specifications. You may have to invite several more participants to fill any gaps that you discover. For example, you may find that you have too few participants from rural schools, or too few African American participants. It may take several additional rounds of invitations and responses to meet your specifications.

3.8.3 How Many Participants?

In some rare situations, there may be only a small number of qualified participants and you may be able to include all or almost all of them in your cutscore study. If the only people you can add as participants are clearly less qualified than the people you already have, there is little point in adding people. Usually, however, there are many more qualified participants to choose from than you can possibly include in your study. In such a case, how many participants should you select? If you have too few, the process may be greatly influenced by one or two individuals with extreme opinions. In this respect, the more participants, the better. Also, the more participants you have, the easier it becomes to represent the important constituencies among the participants. But each additional participant adds to the cost of the study, and the more participants you already have, the less you will gain from adding one more participant.

In general, the more controversial the situation, the more participants you will need. On balance, we suggest that you use about 12–18 participants per

> **...use about 12–18 participants per panel.**

panel. Even though any such number is arbitrary, we suggest 8 as a minimum number of participants in a cutscore study for a test used to make important decisions.[9]

We recommend that you invite more participants than you actually need because not all of those who are invited will agree to participate, not all of those who agree to participate will be able to attend the meeting, and it is possible that not all of those who attend will be able to complete the task. The fewer participants you plan to have, the more important it becomes to have some "extra" participants available to cover attrition. For example, if you plan to have 18 participants, the loss of a few may be acceptable.[10] If you plan to have only 12 participants, the loss of a few can jeopardize your study.

3.9 Find Out How Policymakers Will Treat the Results of the Cutscore Study

The policymakers who have the authority to set the operational cutscores tend to view their role in one of two ways. In one

---

[9] We selected 8 not for psychometric reasons, but because our lawyer was reluctant to defend a cutscore based on fewer than 8 participants. Some facilitators have refused to do a Bookmark study with fewer than 12 participants.

[10] The loss of a few participants may not be acceptable if they are all from the same demographic group and you have no other participants from that group.

view, the policymakers take responsibility for setting the cutscores. They use the cutscores resulting from the cutscore meeting as only one of the different sources of information that they take into account in choosing the operational cutscores. The policymakers may pay as much attention as they desire to other factors such as the consequences of using the cutscores, the relative harm caused by the two types of misclassifications, the relationships of the cutscores with other relevant data, or the need to obtain consistent results across grades in a school setting. The operational cutscores set by the policymakers can differ greatly from the recommended cutscores that resulted from the cutscore study.

In the other view, the policymakers give a great deal of weight to the cutscores recommended by the participants in the cutscore study. The policymakers may, for reasons such as those listed above, adjust the recommended cutscores. They tend to do so only within a small range of points, however.

It is important to find out how the policymakers will treat the cutscores that you provide so you can inform the participants in the cutscore study. If the participants believe that the policymakers will make only small adjustments to the cutscores that the participants recommend, and then later discover that the policymakers greatly revised the recommended cutscores, the participants may feel that you misled them. They may believe that they wasted their time and effort in the cutscore meeting. They may attack the operational cutscores as not representing the views of the participants in the cutscore study. If the participants at the cutscore meeting criticize the operational cutscores, it will be difficult to defend those cutscores.

> *Training participants is a crucial step in helping to ensure that the cutscores the participants set are meaningful.*

3.10 Train the Participants

Regardless of the cutscore method you choose, at least some part of the task is likely to be unfamiliar to your participants. Training participants is a crucial step in helping to ensure that the cutscores the participants set are meaningful.

3.10.1 General Training

Training the participants is so important that you should work from a script or a detailed outline to ensure that you cover everything that you planned to cover. Some of the training is specific to the method of setting cutscores that has been selected. Many important aspects of the training, however, apply to all of the methods of setting cutscores and we will discuss those aspects in this part of the manual.

We suggest that, before the meeting, you distribute to the participants general information about cutscores and specific information about the method to be used. Not all of the participants will read the materials before the meeting, but usually enough of them will

> *...all methods will require at least half a day of training. Some methods require more than half a day to complete all aspects of the training.*

do so to justify the effort. The time required for training will depend, in part, on the cutscore method for which the participants are being trained. In our experience, however, all methods will require at least half a day of training. Some methods require more than half a day to complete all aspects of the training.

We think the participants can do a better job if they understand why they are doing things and are not just mechanically following a set of directions. Therefore, you should inform the participants of the purpose for using cutscores, and what will happen to test takers who are in each performance level. Similarly, we believe that, in addition to learning the mechanics of the particular method they will be using, the participants should learn about the judgmental nature of cutscores and the two types of misclassifications. They should discuss which type of misclassification is more harmful and how much more harmful it is than the other type of misclassification. They should become familiar with the meanings of the performance levels and with the relevant performance level descriptors.

For many methods you will have to explain the meaning of borderline performance (discussed in section 3.10.2) for each of the performance level descriptors you will be using. Tell the participants about the test development process (e.g., what the test is intended to measure and how the questions were developed and selected for the test). In addition, discuss any data they will be receiving about test takers' performance on the test questions and about the anticipated effects of using the cutscores that they might choose. Teach the participants how to interpret the data that you will provide.

Give the participants an overview of the schedule for the entire cutscore session, and describe each of the tasks they will be performing. Point out when the breaks are scheduled to occur. Tell the participants how their individual judgments will be combined to set the group's cutscore. Make clear to the participants that the operational cutscore must be set by policymakers with the legal authority to do so. Make sure the participants are aware that the operational cutscore may differ from the one they recommend.

Participants should be familiar with the test on which cutscores are to be set. Often, the best way to have participants become familiar with the test is to have them actually take the test and answer the questions as part of their training. Participants who have not attempted to answer the test questions on their own are likely to think the test is easier than it actually is. It is far easier to agree with an answer you are told is correct than it is to make a correct response on your own.

If you think the participants may be concerned about having to take the test, tell them that nobody else will see their answers. Make clear that the participants are taking the test only to have a better appreciation of what it is like to try to answer each question. After the participants have taken the test, give them the correct answers and allow them to check their own answers and raise any concerns they may have about the test.

Sometimes, however, it is not appropriate to have the participants take the test. If the participants are already familiar with the test, having them take it is not a productive use of time. Another situation in which it is best not to require participants to take the test arises when you have reason to think that taking the test will annoy or anger the participants and make it more difficult to obtain their cooperation during the remainder of the cutscore study. For example, one of us set cutscores on an occupational test using job incumbents as participants. They believed that taking the test and performing poorly would place their jobs at risk, regardless of assurances to the contrary. Some of the participants threatened to leave the study rather than take the test. In those circumstances, it was clearly better not to administer the test than to administer it.

If you choose not to administer the test, be sure to give participants a chance to read through the test (if they are not already familiar with it). If you choose not to administer the test because of the time involved, consider administering a representative subset of the questions. In any case, make sure that the participants understand that their task at the meeting is to provide the judgments necessary to set a cutscore, not to review and improve the test. For secure tests, have the participants sign a non-disclosure agreement before they take or read the test. (A sample non-disclosure agreement is available in the Appendix).

Keep in mind that at the start of the process of setting cutscores many participants are uncomfortable with the idea that the cutscore is based on their judgments. They may ask why we do not simply calculate the cutscore or use the cutscore from a neighboring state. Help the participants to understand that *all* cutscores are based on judgments, and that these judgments should be linked to the specific content and questions of the assessment or to the performance of actual test takers. Explain to the participants that they were chosen because of their knowledge and experience. Policymakers and statisticians rarely understand exactly what test takers of differing ability levels can do. Nor can they determine the knowledge and skills that are required to answer a test question. Nor do they know what knowledge and skills are required to protect the public from harm in the practice of a profession, or what students in a particular grade are expected to know and be able to do. The expertise of the participants is required for those tasks. Explain that your job is to train the participants to apply their special knowledge and skills appropriately to obtain the cutscores.

3.10.2 Training in Defining Borderline Performance

Many methods of setting cutscores depend to some extent on the concept of *borderline* performance. It is essential for some methods and can help participants make better distinctions among performance levels in other methods. Strictly speaking, the borderline is the point along a continuum of performance where the worst performance that still belongs in a performance level and the best performance that is not yet quite good enough for the performance level become indistinguishable from each other.

In our experience, participants have difficulty understanding the concept of borderline performance as the transition point between performance levels. They find it much easier to think only about the weakest performance that belongs in a performance level. The weakest performance that belongs in a performance level is, however, indistinguishable from borderline performance. Therefore, when you talk to participants about borderline performance, we recommend that you focus on the weakest performance that belongs in the performance level. Some of the early writers about methods of setting cutscores used phrases such as "barely passing," "minimally acceptable," and "minimally competent," to refer to the borderline test taker.

Some participants become confused because, logically, each performance level has two borderlines, one at the bottom of the performance level and one at the top. In common usage, however, the borderline *always* refers to the bottom of the performance level, the worst performance that just barely belongs in the performance level. It may help the participants if you address this point directly.

The reason for setting cutscores is to distinguish among performance levels. To do that, it is necessary to specify the differences in what test takers know and can do that indicate a shift from one performance level to the next. For example, to distinguish between Basic and Proficient essays, it does not help to describe the very best Proficient essay. It does not even help much to describe the typical Proficient essay. To make the distinction, it is necessary to describe the worst essay that should be classified as Proficient rather than Basic.

To define borderline knowledge and skills for a performance level, make sure the participants understand what the test measures and how the test scores will be used. Make sure the participants understand the performance level descriptor and agree on examples of what people in the performance level can and cannot do. Then ask the participants to describe, in their own words, a person whose knowledge and skills are just barely good enough to place the person in that performance level. The participants may find it convenient to describe the performance of specific people they know, whom they would consider borderline.

You can help the process along by asking appropriate questions. For example, if the test is a reading comprehension test that is being used to identify high school seniors who are Proficient in reading, you might ask, "Would the borderline test taker be able to find specific information in a newspaper article? To distinguish statements of fact from statements of opinion in the article? Would the borderline test taker be able to recognize the main idea of a paragraph in the article, stated in different words? How complex an article would the borderline test taker be able to comprehend?"

Commonly, the description of borderline performance is developed by the participants when they meet to set cutscores. You may, however, choose to have the people who write the performance level descriptors also describe borderline performance for each level. If you come to the cutscore meeting with the completed descriptions of borderline performance, check to be sure that the participants understand what test takers who are at the borderline of a performance level know and can do. One way to do that is to see if the participants agree in classifying examples of behavior as above or below the borderline.

If you define borderline performance at the cutscore meeting, allow the participants plenty of time to decide on the meaning of borderline performance and to agree on examples. When the

> **You may have to remind participants several times during the cutscore study to focus on borderline performance.**

participants have agreed on a definition, write it down, complete with examples, so you will have a statement you can refer to during the process of setting cutscores.

In our experience, participants often revert to discussions of "my students" or of the average performer within a level rather than the borderline performer. You may have to remind participants several times during the cutscore study to focus on borderline performance. Participants who give ratings that are very different from those of their colleagues may need to be reminded of the agreed upon definition of borderline performance.

3.10.3 Training for a Specific Method

Participants will have to be trained to apply the method of setting cutscores that you have chosen. Many of the methods require the participants to learn new concepts and to make unfamiliar and difficult judgments. You will be able to base your training on our overview of the method you will use and on our list of procedures for implementing the method. Our manual has been written for you, however, not for the participants. We do not recommend copying our lists of procedures verbatim for the participants.

3.10.4 Concluding Training

The training should conclude with a realistic practice session in which you can observe whether or not the participants are applying the method correctly. We recommend practicing not only the judgments but also the discussion and use of any data of the type you plan to provide. Give participants a chance to see how their responses will be aggregated and have them spend some time discussing any disagreement in their judgments. Show them examples of the types of data they will see during the study. If the data are derived from test takers who differ from the expected operational test takers, tell the participants about the differences. The more of the process that the participants can practice ahead of time, the more likely you are to identify and correct any misunderstandings before they have a chance to influence the operational judgments.

You should not start the operational judgment portion of the study until all of the participants state that they have a clear understanding of the task and are ready to proceed.

You should not start the operational judgment portion of the study until all of the participants state that they have a clear understanding of the task and are ready to proceed. We recommend obtaining a signed statement from each participant, indicating his or her readiness or lack of readiness to proceed, and stating any areas in which further training is required. We often find that when we ask the questions orally, the participants nod and say they understand. When we ask the participants to complete a written statement, however, they are more likely to indicate areas in which their understanding is inadequate.

Although you may think all issues have been resolved at the conclusion of the training, the statements may reveal a need for further training in one or more steps of the participants' task. We also recommend obtaining an evaluation of the various aspects of the training. The evaluation forms should be anonymous.

Collect and review the evaluation forms and the readiness statements before asking the participants to work on the operational materials. Be prepared to offer help to any participants who indicate they are not ready to proceed. Try to schedule the completion of the readiness statements and the evaluation forms just before a break in the training (e.g., lunch), so that you have time to analyze the responses and prepare additional training materials as needed. We recommend that no participant do operational work until he or she has indicated readiness to proceed, in a signed statement. Retain the readiness statements until your lawyer says they may be discarded.

We strongly recommend that you try out the training process on a small sample of people like the participants so you can evaluate its effectiveness, make revisions as necessary, and estimate more accurately the time that should be set aside for training the participants.

3.11 Comply with the AERA, APA, NCME Standards Related to Cutscores

Standards for Educational and Psychological Testing is a joint publication of three major professional organizations concerned with testing: the American Educational Research Association (AERA), the American Psychological Association (APA), and the National Council on Measurement in Education (NCME). This publication presents rules and guidelines for test publishers and test users that cover many aspects of educational, occupational, and psychological testing.

You should know about these standards and strive to follow them because they represent the consensus of the major measurement organizations about good practices. If there is litigation concerning your cutscores (or other aspects of the test), the plaintiff's attorneys are likely to try to show that you did not follow the AERA, APA, NCME *Standards*.

We discuss only those standards that are most relevant to cutscores and their use. Many other standards will apply to other aspects of the test you are using. If it has not yet been

58

done, we suggest that you have a qualified person evaluate your test with respect to the *Standards*.

Each of the standards most closely related to cutscores is summarized below, with a brief explanation of how you can meet each standard. You should also obtain a copy of the *Standards for Educational and Psychological Testing* and read the complete text of each of these standards and the explanatory paragraphs that follow each one.[11] We think that if you follow the advice offered in this manual, you are likely to be in compliance with the standards related to setting cutscores.

According to Standard 1.7, if you use expert judgments to set cutscores, you should describe the procedures for selecting the experts and for eliciting their judgments. Your description should include the experts' qualifications, the training they received, how they interacted and influenced each other, and how strongly they agreed with each other. You should meet this standard if you follow our recommendations in section 7.2 about documenting the cutscore study.

Standard 2.14 says that you should report the standard error of measurement[12] of the test scores, in the portion of the score scale near each cutscore. Your statistician will be able to calculate the standard error of measurement in the part(s) of the score scale in which the cutscore(s) are located. Standard 2.14 takes account of the fact that the standard error of measurement is not the same in all parts of the score scale.

Standard 2.15 requires you to estimate and report the percent of test takers classified the same way on repeated measures. This standard deals with the reliability of classification. For example, if test takers are classified as Proficient, what percent of them would be classified the same way if you gave a different form of the test (assuming no instruction on what the test

---

[11] The standards discussed in this manual are from the 1999 edition of the *Standards*. If a newer edition of the *Standards* is available, please read the standards related to cutscores in that edition.

[12] The standard error of measurement is a statistic that describes the extent to which test scores can be expected to vary because of differences in such factors as the specific questions in different forms of the test, or the leniency or rigor of different scorers.

measures between administrations), or if the constructed-response questions were scored by different people? You probably will not have data from the same test takers responding to alternate forms of the test, but your statistician should be able to estimate these percentages on the basis of data from test takers who have taken only a single form of the test.[13]

Standard 4.4 says, in part, that if any score interpretations are based on cutscores, you need to "support" those interpretations. The steps described in this manual and the documentation we suggest will provide the information you need to support score interpretations based on cutscores.

Standard 4.11 deals with equating, the statistical adjustment for differences in difficulty among different forms of the same test. If you are using two or more forms of a test interchangeably with the same cutscore, the scores on those forms should be equated. If your test forms are equated, your statistician should calculate the standard error of equating in the region of the cutscore because that is the part of the score scale where important decisions are being made about test takers.

Standard 4.19 requires you to document the rationale and procedures for setting cutscores. You will meet this standard if you follow our recommendations in section 7.2, *Document the Cutscore Study.*

Standard 4.20 says that, if it is possible to do so, you should set cutscores using data on the relationship of test scores to relevant criteria. This standard states a preference for cutscores based on criterion data such as performance on the job or performance in school. However, Standard 4.20 also states that good cutscore studies based on judgments about questions are preferable to "an empirical study with an inadequate criterion measure or other deficiencies." If it is possible to do so, use a cutscore method based on the relevant performance of real test takers. If you have good reasons to do otherwise, it would be a good idea to document those reasons, in case you are faulted for lack of compliance with Standard 4.20.

---

[13] For further information, ask your statistician to refer to Livingston and Lewis (1995), cited in *Further Reading.*

According to Standard 4.21, if judgments of test questions or test performances are used, the judgmental process should be designed so that participants can "bring their knowledge and experience to bear in a reasonable way." The standard further recommends giving participants, "practice in judging task difficulty with feedback on accuracy, the experience of actually taking a form of the test, feedback on the failure rates entailed by provisional standards, and other forms of information." We believe that any of the question-judgment or performance-judgment methods described in this manual, if implemented as we have recommended, will meet this standard.

Standard 6.5 is very straightforward. If cutscores are used to interpret scores, the test manual should include the cutscores.

Standard 6.12 is much like Standard 6.5, but it applies when the interpretation of the test score is made by a computer algorithm rather than by a person. The person who uses the computer-generated interpretation should be told what the cutscores are and how they were generated.

Standard 13.6 says, in part, that if alternative measures are allowed for promotion or graduation tests, the cutscores should be equivalent in terms of rigor. The intent of the standard is that the alternative test should be a different method of determining whether or not a student has the required knowledge and skills, not a method of passing students who lack the required knowledge and skills.

According to Standard 14.17, you should not use the cutscore on a licensing test for the purpose of regulating the proportion of people passing the test. For example, you should not raise the cutscore for the purpose of restricting access to the occupation and reducing competition. The cutscore should be based on "the knowledge and skills necessary for acceptable performance."

4. OVERVIEWS OF METHODS OF SETTING CUTSCORES

This section contains brief descriptions of various methods of setting cutscores. The purpose of this section is to familiarize you with different ways of setting cutscores and the advantages and disadvantages of each method. This section, however, does not contain sufficient procedural detail to allow you to run cutscore studies using the methods. After you familiarize yourself with the various methods, read section 5 to help you select an appropriate method. Then consult section 6 for the detailed procedures required to use the method you have chosen.

We are indebted to the people who originated, introduced, or described the methods that we discuss: William. H. Angoff, Luz Bay, Cees H. Beuk, Robert L. Ebel, Steven Ferrara, Donald Ross Green, Ronald K. Hambleton, Willem K. Hofstee, James C. Impara, Richard M. Jaeger, Eugene Johnson, Stuart R. Kahl, Neil M. Kingston, Daniel M. Lewis, Howard C. Mitzel, Leo Nedelsky, Richard J. Patz, Mary J. Pitoniak, Barbara. S. Plake, and Kevin Sweeney. The citations for the methods are listed in the section *Further Reading*.

4.1 Methods Based On Judgments of Test Questions

Nearly all of the methods that depend on judgments of test questions are based on the idea that that an appropriate cutscore would be the test score expected of a typical borderline test taker, one whose knowledge and skills are just barely good enough to be included in a proficiency level. We determine this cutscore by making judgments about the expected performance of a borderline test taker on the test questions. The expected score for a borderline test taker is a logical place for a cutscore, because any test taker with borderline or better proficiency would be expected to score at or above the cutscore, while any test taker with less-than-borderline proficiency would be expected to score below the cutscore. Of course, not every borderline test taker would get this exact score every time he or she takes the test. Rather, this expected score represents the score that is believed to be typical of a borderline test taker's performance.

4.1.1 The Angoff Method [14, 15]

Overview

In this very widely used and well-researched method, participants are asked to state the probability that a borderline test taker would answer each test question correctly. If the test is scored by awarding one point for each correct answer, then the probability that a test taker would answer the question correctly is equal to the test taker's expected score on that question.[16] If you add the expected scores on all the questions, you have the test taker's expected score on the whole test. Therefore, you can find the expected score for a borderline test taker if you know the probability that a borderline test taker will answer each question correctly. The sum of a participant's judgments about the probability that a borderline test taker will answer each question correctly is that participant's estimate of the cutscore.

The group's estimate of the cutscore is calculated by averaging the individual participants' cutscores, using the mean, the trimmed mean, or the median. When you have collected the judgments, computed the resulting score for each participant, and combined the results, you will have a group judgment of the score that a borderline test taker would be expected to get on the test.

Advantages and Disadvantages

The Angoff method is convenient, very widely used, and has been the subject of a great deal of research. If any method of

---

[14] Angoff attributed the method to Ledyard Tucker, but we follow common usage in calling it the Angoff method.

[15] The literature on cutscores has many references to the "Modified Angoff method," but there is no single "Modified Angoff method." Angoff described his method in only a few sentences, giving no details on how to implement the method. Some people who add features beyond those described by Angoff call their cutscore studies "Modified Angoff methods," but there are many different versions of the method sharing that name.

[16] For questions scored on a scale rather than correct or incorrect (i.e., questions on which the test taker can receive partial credit), use the Angoff Mean Estimation method discussed next.

setting cutscores can be called an established, recognized method, it is the Angoff method. However, it shares the problem of all of the methods based on judgments of how borderline test takers would perform. The judgments required of participants are unfamiliar and difficult to make. The results can be divorced from reality unless real data about test taker performance are shared with the participants (which we strongly recommend).

Some researchers have said that the judgments required by the Angoff method (and all other question-judgment methods) are too hard for the participants to make, but the method has been defended by other researchers. In our experience, participants may express some initial discomfort with the Angoff judgments, but we have never had a participant say after training that the judgments were too hard to make.

4.1.2 The Angoff Mean Estimation Method

Overview

The Angoff method, as described above, is limited to questions scored correct or incorrect, 0 or 1. However, the Angoff method can be extended to work with constructed-response questions that are scored with more than one point per question (e.g., with possible scores of 1–3, 0–6, 1–10, 0–25). Instead of asking participants to state the probability that borderline test takers would get the question right, simply ask the participants to estimate the average score that a large group of borderline test takers would obtain on the question. This average score does not have to be an integer. For example, if an essay is scored on a scale from 1–6, one participant might estimate that a group of borderline test takers would obtain an average score of 2.5. Another participant might estimate the average score of borderline test takers to be 3.2, and so forth.

Though it may seem different, the Angoff procedure for constructed-response questions is mathematically the same as the Angoff procedure for multiple-choice questions. When participants estimate the probability that a borderline test taker will answer a multiple-choice question correctly, they are also estimating the average score that a large group of borderline test takers would obtain on the question. For example, if the participants estimate that the probability of a borderline test taker answering a multiple choice question correctly is .50, that means 50 percent of a large group of borderline test takers would answer the question correctly. Half would score 0 on the question and half would score 1. Therefore, the average score would be .50.

As in the Angoff method, sum the estimated scores for each participant to get each participant's cutscore. Then use the mean, median, or trimmed mean to get the group's estimate of the cutscore.

Advantages and Disadvantages

The Angoff Mean Estimation method shares the advantages and disadvantages of the Angoff method with the additional advantage of being applicable to constructed-response questions on which the test taker can get partial credit for a partially correct answer. If a test contains both constructed-response and multiple-choice questions, you can combine the Angoff and Angoff Mean Estimation methods in the same cutscore study.

4.1.3 The Angoff Yes or No Method

Overview

The popular Angoff method explained above was first described in a brief footnote in a chapter that Angoff wrote for a book about educational measurement. The footnote referred to a paragraph in the body of the chapter. In that paragraph Angoff suggested a method for setting a cutscore by keeping the borderline person in mind and judging whether or not such a person would get each question right or wrong.

In effect, the Yes or No method is just like the popular Angoff method except that the only allowable probabilities are zero and one.

Advantages and Disadvantages

It is easier and quicker for the participants to make a yes or no judgment than it is to estimate a probability for each question. Furthermore, the method is easier to explain to participants than the more commonly used Angoff method. A disadvantage is that the method does not allow participants to make all of the distinctions they may desire to make and may be able to make. For example, a participant may feel strongly that a borderline test taker has a probability of .80 of answering one question correctly and a probability of .40 of answering another question correctly, but the method does not allow either of those estimates to be made. In the Yes or No method, the estimated probabilities are pushed to extreme values. The estimated probability of .40 would become 0 and the estimated probability of .80 would become 1.

4.1.4 The Nedelsky Method

Overview

The Nedelsky method can be used only with multiple-choice tests because it requires a judgment about each possible wrong answer. The participant's task is to look at the question and eliminate the wrong answers that a borderline test taker would be able to recognize as wrong. For example, consider the following question.

> Which of the following is the first thing you should do to help a person who just received a slight wound on the hand from a dog bite?
> A. Apply a tourniquet around the person's arm and tighten it until the bleeding stops.
> B. Pack the hand in ice to alleviate pain and reduce swelling.
> C. Wash the bitten area with soap and warm water.
> D. Apply pressure to the wound with a clean dressing.

A participant might decide that the borderline test taker would be able to eliminate wrong answers A and B because they are both harmful to the bitten person. Wrong answer D is not harmful and is a reasonable thing to do eventually, but it is not what should be done first. The participant might decide, however, that the choice between correct answer C and wrong answer D is too difficult for the borderline test taker. The participant would then identify answers A and B as being so clearly wrong that the borderline test taker would be able to recognize them as wrong.

The probability of a correct response to a question is 1 divided by the number of remaining choices. In the example above, the borderline test taker is able to eliminate two choices (A and B). Because the question has four choices, there are two choices remaining (C and D). The probability of a correct response is therefore 1 divided by 2, or .50. If the question had a total of five choices, eliminating two choices would leave three remaining. The probability of a correct response would be 1 divided by 3, or .33. After the probability of a correct response for each question has been calculated, add all of the probabilities to obtain the participant's estimate of the cutscore. Find the average cutscore by using the mean, median, or trimmed mean.

Advantages and Disadvantages

The Nedelsky method is most useful in disciplines in which the wrong answers to a question really differ in their consequences. For example, in a medical context, some of the wrong answers may describe treatments that will harm the patient, while other wrong answers describe treatments that are not harmful. A participant might expect the borderline test taker to know enough to eliminate the harmful choices, but not enough to eliminate the other incorrect choices. More generally, the method can be used with any multiple-choice test in which the wrong answer choices differ significantly in their attractiveness to test takers who do not know the correct answer.

The Nedelsky method shares the general disadvantage of all of the question-judgment methods. It can be divorced from reality and the judgments are unfamiliar to the participants. An additional disadvantage of the method is that it is time consuming because participants have to make a decision about every wrong answer in every question. Furthermore, only a few different correct-answer probabilities can result from each participant's judgments of each question. If the participant decides that the borderline test taker can eliminate all the wrong answer choices, the correct-answer probability is 1.00. If the participant decides that the borderline test taker can eliminate all but one of the wrong answer choices, the correct-answer probability is .50. Nothing between .50 and 1.00 is possible. This feature can cause the cutscores produced by the Nedelsky method to be lower than those produced by other methods based on judgments about test questions. The reduction in the number of probabilities available may make it difficult to use the Nedelsky method for setting multiple cutscores on the same test.

4.1.5 The Ebel Method

Overview

The Ebel method is a two-stage procedure. Each participant first classifies the questions into groups. The participant then makes a single judgment for each group of questions, specifying the probability that a borderline test taker would answer each of the questions in the group correctly. The participant specifies the same probability for all of the questions in the group. The classification of questions into groups is based on two kinds of judgments about each question: a judgment of its difficulty and a judgment of its relevance (or importance). Ebel suggested three difficulty levels, labeled "easy," "medium," and "hard," and four relevance categories, labeled "essential," "important," "acceptable," and "questionable." You may use other labels and different numbers of categories if they are more appropriate for the test under consideration.

To get the participant's cutscore, start with the first group of questions and multiply the participant's estimated probability for that group by the number of questions in the group. Do this for each group of questions and then add up all of the products. To get the group's cutscore, average the participants' cutscores using the mean, the median, or the trimmed mean.

Advantages and Disadvantages

The participants have to make only 12 judgments (if there are 12 groups of questions) of the probability that a borderline test taker would answer questions correctly, regardless of the number of questions in the test. Participants may find it easier to think about the percentage of correct answers to a group of questions than to think about the probability of a correct answer to a single question.

The classification by relevance encourages participants to consider the importance of the knowledge and skills being measured by the questions. The Ebel method shares the weakness of all methods based on the judgments of test questions. Furthermore, the multiple judgments required can be time consuming. There is less research on the Ebel method than there is on the Angoff method.

4.1.6 The Bookmark Method

Overview

The Bookmark method was developed to be used with tests that are scored using Item Response Theory (IRT).[17] It is now one of the most widely used cutscore-setting methods for state K–12 assessments. To use this method as it was designed, you must have a test that was calibrated using IRT. You must also have a statistician available who knows how to use IRT and who has access to the software required for the necessary calculations.

The participant is given a special test booklet called an *Ordered Item Booklet* that displays the questions in order of difficulty from easy to hard. The participant's task is to place a bookmark at the spot that separates the questions into two groups—a group of easier questions that the borderline test taker would probably answer correctly (with *probably* meaning a chance of at least 2 out of 3 or .67), and a group of harder questions that the borderline test taker would probably not answer correctly (i.e., the test taker would have a probability of less than .67 of answering correctly). After the participant has made this placement of the bookmark, the statistician can determine the expected test score for a borderline test taker.

The IRT estimates of question difficulty and test taker ability can be placed on the same numerical scale. Because the questions in the Ordered Item Booklet are listed in order of difficulty, every possible placement of the bookmark corresponds to a point on the difficulty scale. In the Bookmark method, the point indicates the ability of a borderline test taker who has a two-thirds probability (known as the response probability) of correctly answering a question of that difficulty. The statistician can then use IRT to compute the expected test score for a test taker of

---

[17] An item is what psychometricians call a test question. Item Response Theory (IRT) is a mathematical procedure for estimating the probability that a test taker will answer a test question correctly. The basic theory (there are variations) states that this probability depends on the ability of the test taker and on the difficulty (and possibly other characteristics) of the test question. IRT yields numerical estimates of each test taker's ability and of the difficulty of each test question.

that ability.[18] The expected test score of a borderline test taker is the cutscore implied by the placement of the bookmark.

Advantages and Disadvantages

An advantage of the Bookmark method is its efficiency in setting two or more cutscores on the same test. For example, the cutscore between Basic and Proficient and the cutscore between Proficient and Advanced can be set from judgments collected at the same time. Participants seem to understand their task. Teachers like the focus on the knowledge and skills that the questions are measuring and appreciate seeing the items ordered by student performance. This method works well with both multiple-choice and constructed-response questions. The Bookmark method requires less data entry than other question-judgment methods as the statistician has to enter only one number for each participant for each cutscore.

One disadvantage is the pre-work needed to produce the Ordered Item Booklets. To use the Bookmark method as we have described it, all of the questions must be IRT-calibrated in advance of the cutscore study. The statistician must prepare complete tables of the cutscores associated with each possible bookmark placement for use in the cutscore study.

Another disadvantage is that participants have difficulty understanding and using the Response Probability. It is highly unlikely that any participant can differentiate among the response probabilities of .65, .67, or .70. Another concern is that Item Response Theory can have counterintuitive results for people who are not familiar with it. For example, many participants misinterpret the number of questions before the bookmark as the number-right cutscore. That is, they think if they place the bookmark on question 18, the test taker will need to answer 17 questions correctly to pass. Because of the transformation of question difficulty to ability level, the actual raw score cutscore rarely matches the number of questions before the bookmark. Furthermore, participants are often curious about IRT and it can be difficult to explain IRT to people who are not familiar with the mathematical concepts involved.

---

[18] The statistician can use IRT to compute the borderline test taker's probability of answering each question correctly. The sum of the probabilities is the expected test score for a borderline test taker.

The ordering of the questions by difficulty can change when the test is administered to a different group of test takers at a different time. Because the cutscore depends heavily on the ordering of the questions in the Ordered Item Booklet, this kind of change can leave the cutscore open to challenges. This ordering change is particularly noticeable with a new testing program because the difficulties of the questions change rapidly over time as people discover what is covered by the test and prepare themselves (or their students) accordingly.

Finally, as of the time we are writing this manual, the Bookmark method has not been well-researched, though we expect the popularity of the method will encourage the necessary research in the next few years.

4.1.7 The Item Descriptor Matching Method

Overview

The Item Descriptor Matching method, often called the ID Matching method, requires a test that was calibrated using Item Response Theory (IRT). You must have a statistician available who knows how to use IRT and who has access to the software required for the necessary calculations.

As described for the Bookmark method, an Ordered Item Booklet lists all of the test questions in order of increasing difficulty, as determined in the IRT calibration of the questions. In Item Descriptor Matching, the participants associate each test question in the Ordered Item Booklet with a performance level, using the performance level descriptors and their own determination of what a test taker must know and be able to do to answer the question correctly. Participants match the knowledge and skills required to answer each question to the knowledge and skills required to be in a performance level. For example, if a question requires a test taker to solve a particular type of problem, and the solution of such problems is part of the performance level descriptor for the Advanced Level and not for any lower level, the participant would match the question with the Advanced level.

The participants write the initial of the selected performance level (e.g., Basic, Proficient, or Advanced) next to each question. After matching each question to a performance level, the participants analyze the pattern of matches to determine where the knowledge and skills seem to change from one performance level to the next. Then they draw a cutline[19] between two questions at the point that best represents the borderline between the lower performance level and the next higher performance level. The process is repeated if more than one cutscore has to be set. The cutscore is calculated as in the Bookmark method.

Advantages and Disadvantages

Many of the advantages and disadvantages of Item Descriptor Matching are very similar to those of the Bookmark method and we will not repeat them here. An important advantage of Item Descriptor Matching over the Bookmark method is that the participant's task is one that is familiar to educators and is easy to explain. There is no need to consider a hypothetical test taker, only to match the knowledge and skills required to answer a question to a performance level descriptor. Furthermore, there is no need for the participants to think about a Response Probability which removes a major source of confusion. A disadvantage is that the method has not been widely used, and has been little researched.

4.2 Methods Based on Profiles of Scores

The *profile* is the test taker's pattern of scores on separate parts of a test. (If the scores on different parts of a test are reported separately, they are often called *subscores*.) If the test taker's scores are the same on all parts of the test, the profile will be flat. If the test taker scored high on some parts of the test and low on other parts of the test, the

> **Profiles are useful if there is meaningful information in the differences among the subscores in the profile.**

profile will be uneven. Profiles are useful if there is meaningful information in the differences among the subscores in the profile.

4.2.1 The Performance Profile Method

Overview

The Performance Profile method works best with tests consisting of small numbers of performance questions or tasks

---

[19] Cutline is the preferred term in Item Descriptor Matching studies because the participant literally draws a line between two questions to indicate his or her choice of a cutscore.

72

(usually three to eight). Tests used with very young test takers and tests used with special populations, such as people with significant cognitive disabilities, often consist of a few performance questions, as do some tests for technical occupations.

The participants become familiar with the meaning of each score in the profile. The participants review individual test taker score profiles, each profile showing a test taker's scores on the individual performance questions. The profiles are arranged in order of their total scores, from lowest to highest in an Ordered Profile Booklet. The participants then examine the ordered profiles and select the first profile that is indicative of borderline performance at a performance level. For example, a participant may decide that a profile of 4, 6, 3, 5 with a total score of 18 is indicative of borderline Proficient performance.

There will probably be several different profiles with the same total score as the selected profile. Participants next examine all of the profiles provided with the same total score as the selected profile. To continue the example, profiles of 9, 2, 1, 6 and 5, 4, 5, 4 have the same total score as the selected profile. If all of the profiles at the selected total score are judged to represent Proficient performance, the selected total score is the participant's cutscore for the Proficient performance level.

A participant may decide, however, that some of the profiles at the same total score represent Proficient performance, but others are below Proficient. For example, a participant may decide that 5, 4, 5, 4 represents Proficient performance, but 9, 2, 1, 6 does not. In that case, the participant has to decide whether it is preferable to treat all of the profiles at that total score as Proficient or to treat all of the profiles at that total score as below Proficient.[20]

If a participant believes that it is preferable to treat all of the profiles at a total score as below Proficient, the participant

---

[20] It may be helpful to re-read *There Will Be Misclassifications* (section 2.4) and *Some Misclassifications Are More Harmful than Others* (section 2.5) before using this method.

repeats the process at the next higher total score, and so on until a total score is found at which the participant decides that it is preferable to treat all of the profiles at that total score level as Proficient.

This method allows participants to evaluate different ways of obtaining the same total score and to decide if all of the ways of obtaining the same score are good enough to be acceptable within a performance level or not. The total score of the profile selected by the participant is the participant's cutscore. Use the mean, the median, or the trimmed mean to obtain the group's cutscore for that performance level.

Advantages and Disadvantages

An advantage of the Performance Profile method is that the profiles can give participants a better view of test taker performance on the whole test than is obtained by considering each question in isolation. The Performance Profile method can be used to set cutscores for two or more performance levels at the same time. IRT is not required for the Performance Profile method and there are no probability decisions that must be made.

A disadvantage of the Performance Profile method is the amount of preparation needed to select the profiles at each score level and to create the Ordered Profile Booklets. The method can become cumbersome if there are more than seven or so separately scored questions. The Performance Profile method is fairly new and is not yet well researched.

4.2.2 The Dominant Profile Method

Before you use the Dominant Profile Method, we recommend that you consult with a content expert to make sure that the test content contributing to each subscore is meaningfully different from the test content contributing to each of the other subscores.

Overview

The Dominant Profile method is used when (1) different parts of the test measure different knowledge and skills, (2) separate scores are computed and reported for each part of the test, and (3) there is a reason *not* to have only a single overall cutscore. The outcome of this method is usually not a single cutscore. Usually the method results in a set of decision rules. Those rules can specify separate cutscores for each subscore, or have a single cutscore for the total score and allow high performance on some parts of the test to compensate for low performance on some other parts of the test. The rules may specify some combination of total score and subscore cutscores. If the test does not produce score profiles for individual test takers, there is no reason to use this method.

The participant's task is to become familiar with the meanings of the subscores and to specify rules for determining which combinations of subscores represent acceptable performance and which do not. The rules can combine information from the subscores in various ways, as in the following example:

- No subscore below 10 on any part
- At least one subscore of 15 or higher
- A total score of at least 60 points

Advantages and Disadvantages

The advantage of the method is that it allows for direct conversion of participants' values into a set of decision rules that can incorporate both subscore cutscores and a total score cutscore. This is useful if policymakers do not believe that simpler approaches are suitable.

One disadvantage is that the method can be time-consuming. In some uses of the method described in the professional literature, the participants ran out of time and the work had to be completed by mail. Calculating the impact of complicated score profiles can be difficult, particularly during the limited time available at a cutscore meeting.

A major disadvantage of a decision rule that applies separate cutscores to individual subscores is that the reliability of the overall decision will depend on the reliability of the least reliable of those subscores. Also, complicated decision rules involving combinations of cutscores are difficult to explain and apply.

4.3 Methods Based on Judgments of People or Products

There are several methods of setting cutscores that rely on judgments of either the test takers themselves or of the work they produce. The work may be produced in the normal course of events or in the context of the assessment. For these methods, participants must be able to determine each test taker's knowledge and skills. Participants must also know what level of knowledge and skills a person in each performance level should have, but you can provide that information as part of the training for a cutscore study.

There are several ways for participants to determine a test taker's knowledge and skills.

- Participants can evaluate some product of the test taker's work generated either during a test or in a natural setting. For example, participants may evaluate a response to an essay question, a painting, a welded joint between two steel plates, or a soufflé.

- Participants can evaluate a sample of performance collected in a testing situation or in a natural setting. For example, participants may observe a medical student examine a patient and make a diagnosis, or participants may observe a student driver parallel park a car.

- Participants can evaluate the test taker's performance in a natural setting over an extended period of time. This will often be the case for teachers in a school setting and for supervisors in an occupational setting.

It is not necessary to arrange for observations of everyone who has ever taken the test. What you need is a sample of the test takers or their products. The sample of test takers should have scores spanning all parts of the score range where the cutscore(s) might plausibly be located.

If the participants are teachers judging their students, tell the teachers not to make any judgment of a test taker whose skills they have not had the chance to observe adequately. The same principle applies when you are asking supervisors to judge the workers they supervise.

What if the test itself provides the best available indication of the test takers' skills? In this case, the participants can base their judgments on an observation of the test takers' actual test performance—not the test score, but the performance itself. For example, when an essay test is used to test writing skills, the participants can read the test takers' essays. For a test of foreign-language speaking ability or musical performance, the participants can listen to the actual performance, or a portion of it (either live or recorded).

The judgments must be based on the knowledge and skills the test is intended to measure. These methods will not work well if the judgments of the skills of test takers are affected by factors that are irrelevant to the purpose of the test. For example, teachers who are asked to judge their students' skills in English composition may allow their judgments to be influenced by the students' understanding of literature, their punctuality in completing assignments, their class participation, their behavior in class, and so on. Instructions to the participants can help to reduce the influence of these irrelevant factors. The participants must understand clearly which characteristics of the test takers they should judge and which they should disregard.

The judgments should take into account the conditions under which the performance samples were produced. For example, students who are able to produce well-written papers when given several weeks to complete the assignment, access to reference books and automated spell-checkers may show considerably less writing skill in a 20-minute essay written during a test.

The judgments must reflect the test takers' skills at the time of testing. If the judgments are based on the participants' familiarity with the test takers' knowledge and skills, the judgments should be made as close to the time of testing as possible. If the judgments are based on an observation of the test takers' performance, the performance that the participants observe should occur as close to the time of testing as possible. (If the performance is recorded close to the time of testing, it can be observed and judged at a later time.)

There is one exception to this requirement. If the test is intended to predict the test takers' skills at some future time, then the observations and judgments should be based on the test takers' performance at that future time. For example, if a test is intended to predict success in a training course, the test would be given before the course, but the judgments of the test takers' success would have to be made at the end of the training course.

We strongly recommend that the participants *not* know the test takers' test scores until after the judging process is complete. Avoid giving the participants information that will allow them to infer the test takers' scores. For example, if you number essay responses to help participants identify a particular response, do not number them in order of increasing or decreasing scores. A participant who knows the test takers' scores will find it difficult to avoid being influenced by those scores in making judgments about the test takers. Even if the judgments are based on a performance that is part of the test itself, the participants should base their judgments on the performance itself, not on the test scores. If these cutscore methods are to work, the participants' judgments must not be based on the scores on the test on which the cutscores are to be set.

4.3.1 The Borderline Group Method

Overview

This method is based on the idea that the cutscore should be the score that would be expected from a test taker whose skills are on the borderline of a performance level. In this respect it resembles the methods based on judgments of test questions. However, instead of asking the participants to make educated guesses about the way a borderline test taker would perform, this method calls for the participants to identify actual test takers as borderline in the knowledge and skills the test measures. The participants do not have to judge all of the test takers or even a representative sample of them. They need only identify the ones who, in their judgment, fit the definition of a borderline test taker. You then set the cutscore at the median score (the 50th percentile) of this borderline group.

Advantages and Disadvantages

An important advantage of this method is its simplicity. It is easy to use and easy to explain. It has the advantages of the methods based on judgments of real test takers or real products because it calls for judgments of real people or real things. The main disadvantage of this method is that borderline test takers usually are a small percentage of all the test takers. For example, if you ask teachers to identify students in their classes who are borderline performers, you may have to survey a large number of teachers to obtain a sufficient number of borderline test takers. Furthermore, the participants may have trouble identifying test takers who are truly borderline.

4.3.2 The Contrasting Groups Method

Overview

This method is based on the idea that the test takers at each score level can be divided into two contrasting groups on the basis of judgments of their knowledge and skills: a group that is qualified to belong in a performance level and a group that is not qualified to be in a performance level. For example, you could ask a sample of teachers, who do not know their students' test scores, to identify their students who are performing at the Proficient level in mathematics and those who are performing at the Basic level in mathematics.

Once the teachers have divided the test takers into these two groups, you can obtain the test takers' scores and find the test score that best separates the two groups. To do that, consider the test takers with a particular test score and ask, "What percent of the test takers are Proficient?" If the test score is low, most of the test takers will be in the Basic performance level. As you go up the score scale, the proportion of the test takers who are Proficient will increase. At the lower score levels, the Basic test takers will outnumber the Proficient test takers. At the higher score levels, the Proficient test takers will outnumber the Basic test takers. One reasonable choice for a cutscore would be the score at which 50 percent of the test takers are Proficient because that would represent the borderline of the Proficient performance level.

You can obtain the same kind of judgments about products made by test takers. For example, participants could judge whether essays written by test takers represented writing at the Basic level or writing at the Proficient level. After the participants have classified the essays as Basic or Proficient, you can obtain the scores assigned to the essays. Then, for each score level you can calculate the percent Proficient. As in the judgments of test takers, one reasonable choice for a cutscore would be the score at which 50 percent of the essays are Proficient because that would represent the borderline of the Proficient performance level.

> *Two important advantages of the Contrasting Groups method are that: 1) it is based on judgments about real people or products and 2) the participants are making the kinds of judgments that they know how to make.*

Advantages and Disadvantages

Two important advantages of the Contrasting Groups method are that: 1) it is based on judgments about real people or products and 2) the participants are making the kinds of judgments that they know how to make. The method is also easy to explain. Another important advantage is that the Contrasting Groups method lets you see the effects of setting the cutscore at any location in terms of the misclassifications that will be made. You can adjust the cutscore to minimize the harm caused by the misclassifications if one type of misclassification is worse than the other.

A disadvantage of the Contrasting Groups method is the difficulty of obtaining comparable evaluations of test takers for large jurisdictions such as a state. For example, if all of the eighth grade teachers throughout a state are asked to classify each of their students as Basic, Proficient, or Advanced in reading, it will be very difficult to ensure that all of the teachers are making comparable classifications. It is not difficult, however, to obtain comparable judgments of products produced by test takers from a large jurisdiction. For example, if you were measuring students' writing, you could obtain a statewide sample of students' essays and have the essays all judged by the same group of trained participants.

4.3.3 The Up and Down Modification of the Contrasting Groups Method

Overview

The Up and Down method is a way of focusing the participants' judgments where they will do the most good, in the area of the score scale where the cutscore will be.

A problem that often arises in cutscore studies is the effort and expense involved in getting the participants' judgments. In a Contrasting Groups study, the cost may depend heavily on the number of judgments of individual test takers. The most useful judgments will be those of test takers whose test scores are fairly near the cutscore(s). But until you have collected the judgments, you don't know what part(s) of the score range that will be. Is there a way out of this dilemma? Yes, under two conditions: (1) the test takers take the test before their skills are judged, and (2) the test takers can be selected for judgment one at a time. An example would be a foreign-language speaking test, in which the participants' responses are recorded and available for judgment.

Select a test taker near the point on the score scale where you think the cutscore might be. If the first test taker is judged to be clearly below the Proficient level, for example, select the second test taker from a somewhat higher score level. If the second test taker is judged to be clearly above the Proficient level, select the third test taker from a score level that is lower than that of the second test taker, but higher than that of the first test taker. Continue until the borderline of the performance level is found, where it becomes difficult to decide if the test takers are above or below the Proficient level. At that point about half the test takers will be judged to be Proficient and half will be judged to be below Proficient.

Advantages and Disadvantages

The method has the same advantages and disadvantages as the Contrasting Groups method with the added advantage of focusing the participants' judgments in the area of the cutscore. A disadvantage of the method is that it can be applied only when the test takers' or products' scores are known and you can use those scores to select the test takers or products for judgment.

4.3.4 The Body of Work Method

Overview

The Body of Work method is a Contrasting Groups approach that focuses on categorizing student work rather than the students themselves. The method is designed for tests with performance questions or tasks that yield observable products of a test taker's work, such as essays or recorded speech or musical performances. The method does not work well for tests that include large numbers of multiple-choice questions, but it will work if there are some multiple-choice questions with the performance questions.

A test taker's responses to all of the questions in a test are placed in a Response Booklet. There is a separate booklet for each test taker. The word *booklet* is used very loosely. The Response Booklet could be a booklet of responses to essay questions, or it could be a CD or DVD containing audio or video recordings of a test taker's responses. The Response Booklet could be a portfolio of artwork or a set of x-ray studies. What the Response Booklet must be is a collection of observable responses to (mostly) performance test questions in a format that the participants can conveniently evaluate during the cutscore study.

If the test contains multiple-choice questions, include them in the Response Booklet with the correct answers and the answers the test takers selected. Include the test taker's number correct on the set of multiple-choice questions as well. Inform participants of the weight to be given to the multiple-choice questions in comparison to the weight to be given to the performance questions.

The participant's judgment of each test taker is based on the Response Booklet containing the test taker's responses to all of the questions on the test. The participant makes a single judgment about the entire set of responses in the Response Booklet, matching the knowledge and skills exhibited in the responses to the knowledge and skills required to be in a performance level.

There are usually three iterations of the judgments. The first iteration is a training round, the second is a range-finding round, and the third is a pinpointing round. As the names imply, the range-finding round identifies the part of the score scale in which each cutscore lies, and the pinpointing round identifies the actual cutscore within that part.

The cutscore between two performance levels is chosen by finding the point on the score scale that best distinguishes between the Response Booklets placed in each of the performance levels.

Advantages and Disadvantages

The Body of Work method shares many of the advantages and disadvantages of the Contrasting Groups method. For teachers, the task is familiar. In effect, they are evaluating a test taker's test paper (or other response) and giving it a grade.

The Body of Work method also has its own particular advantages and disadvantages. An advantage is that the participants make decisions based on all of a test taker's responses, the whole "body of work." Multiple rounds help focus participants' judgments on the test takers' responses at those parts of the score scale where the judgments are most useful. A disadvantage of the method is the need to find large samples of Response Booklets in the appropriate parts of the score scale after the range-finding session. There is also a need to copy materials rapidly after the range-finding round has been completed. This can be a real problem if materials other than written materials must be copied.[21] The method can be time consuming and tiring for the participants if the Response Booklets take a long time to evaluate.

4.3.5 The Analytic Judgment Method

Overview

In the Analytic Judgment method, judgments are made on responses to individual questions (or groups of related questions) rather than on a test taker or product as a whole. It was designed to be used with tests made of several essay or performance questions. The method will work for tests that include some multiple choice questions with the performance questions as long as the questions can be grouped into meaningful content clusters.

The Analytic Judgment method begins by asking participants to review samples of test takers' work. It is similar to the Body of Work method, but there are two distinct differences:

1. Participants make judgments on test takers' responses to individual questions or to clusters of related questions rather than to the entire Response Booklet at once, and

2. In addition to classifying a response into a performance level, participants further classify the responses at each performance level into *low*, *middle*, and *high* categories. For example, a response is not simply classified as Proficient. It is, in addition, classified as low Proficient, middle Proficient, or high Proficient.

For each question or group of related questions, the cutscore is the score that most clearly distinguishes between the best responses in the lower performance level and the worst responses in the higher performance level (e.g., between responses classified as high Proficient and responses classified as low Advanced.) Those are the responses that are close to the borderline between the performance levels. The cutscores

---

[21] Some facilitators make multiple copies of all of the sampled Response Booklets in the range of possible cutscores before the cutscore meeting. They prefer the expense of making unused copies to the problems associated with making copies of selected Booklets between the range-finding round and the pinpointing round, during the cutscore study.

for all of questions or all of the groups of questions are summed to get the cutscore for the total test.

Advantages and Disadvantages

The Analytic Judgment method is similar to the Contrasting Groups and Body of Work methods and shares many of their advantages and disadvantages. Participants tend to find this method relatively easy to understand and perform. The cognitive task is familiar to the participants. Participants have tended to reach consensus.

However, this method can be time consuming because of the numbers of responses to be judged and the need to categorize the responses as high, medium or low within a performance level. The task of copying responses for the participants can be difficult and time consuming.

4.4 Methods Based on Judgments about Groups of Test Takers

These methods differ from the Contrasting Groups family of methods because the judgments are made about whole groups of test takers at one time, rather than about individual test takers, one at a time. The first method described in this section is based on judgments about a single group of test takers, preferably a large group. This group is often called the *reference group*. The second method is based on judgments about two reference groups.

The participants must be able to judge how many (or what percentage) of the test takers in the reference group belong in each performance level based on the knowledge and skills the test measures. Therefore, they must know what the test measures and what level of these skills is necessary to be in a performance level. They must also be familiar with the abilities of the reference group, as a group. They do not have to identify specific individuals as belonging to a specific performance level, but they must be able to judge approximately what percent of the group belongs in each performance level.

4.4.1 Judgments about a Reference Group

Overview

The simplest of these methods, and the one with the most obvious justification, is to choose the cutscores that would have placed a specified percentage of the reference group into each performance level. For example, if you have some evidence that 35 percent of the test takers should have been classified as Basic, 45 percent as Proficient, and 20 percent as Advanced, you can find the cutscores that would have produced those results and use them as the cutscores. Judgments of the percentages of the people in the reference group who are in each performance level lead directly to the choice of a set of cutscores. The judgments about the people in the reference group should be based on some type of information other than the test scores.

We recommend using this method if there are naturally occurring groups for whom the necessary judgments are routinely made, such as students who are graded or employees who are evaluated.

Advantages and Disadvantages

The main advantage of this method is that it is firmly grounded in the reality of test takers' performance. It is very unlikely to produce unreasonable and unanticipated results. For that reason, we recommend the use of this method as a reality check on the methods based on judgments about test questions. For example, if you can be fairly sure that 65 to 80 percent of last year's test takers were Proficient or higher, you should be skeptical of any method that produces a cutscore that would have classified only 40 percent of last year's test takers as Proficient or higher.

...if you can be fairly sure that 65 to 80 percent of last year's test takers were Proficient or higher, you should be skeptical of any method that produces a cutscore that would have classified only 40 percent of last year's test takers as Proficient or higher.

The main disadvantage of this method is the difficulty of finding participants qualified to judge what percentage of the test takers in the reference group belong in each performance level. This disadvantage disappears if you have naturally occurring groups for whom the necessary judgments are routinely made.

4.4.2 Judgments about Two Reference Groups

Overview

A method that is based on judgments of two groups of test takers does not require judgments of individual test takers. Instead, you identify a group of persons who can be presumed to be, for example, Proficient and a similar group of persons who can be presumed to be less than Proficient. For example, students who have had the relevant instruction and received acceptable grades and similar students who have had the relevant instruction and received unacceptable grades form useful reference groups. The method rests on the assumption that the people in the reference groups are like the people who will take the operational test.

Advantages and Disadvantages

An advantage of the method is that it is based on the actual performance of real people. It is very efficient to make judgments about a group of test takers as a whole rather than about individual test takers. A disadvantage of the method is that it will *not* necessarily produce the same result as the Contrasting Groups method based on judgments of individual test takers. Therefore, it will not necessarily minimize the number of wrong decisions in the group of test takers the test is intended for.

A major disadvantage is that merely identifying one group as, for example, Proficient and the other as less than Proficient is not very precise. The Proficient group could be far above the borderline, or close to it. The group that is less than Proficient could be very far from proficiency or close to it. Those differences can make a big difference in the placement of the cutscore and the location of the cutscore becomes difficult to specify appropriately.

4.5 Methods Based on Compromises between Absolute and Normative Judgments

One last group of methods, known as compromise methods, represent a compromise between absolute standards and relative standards. These compromise methods typically require two kinds of judgments: (1) judgments of an appropriate cutscore, disregarding the percentages that will be classified into each performance level as a result; (2) judgments of the appropriate percentages of test takers in the performance levels, disregarding the cutscores necessary to produce those percentages. We describe two such methods: the Beuk method and the Hofstee method.[22] Either of these methods can be used to choose more than one cutscore on a test, but the method must be applied separately for each cutscore. We will use the term "pass rate" to refer to the percentage of the test takers whose scores are above the cutscore.

4.5.1 The Beuk Method

In the Beuk method each participant specifies both a passing score and a pass rate. Beuk does not specify how the participant is to specify a passing score, but we suggest using any of the methods we have described that provide a cutscore for each participant. The underlying principle is that the two types of judgments are weighted in a way that gives greater weight to the type of judgment on which there is greater agreement among the participants. This weighting, combined with the test score data, leads to a single cutscore for the group of participants.

4.5.2 The Hofstee Method

In Hofstee's method, each participant specifies the highest and lowest acceptable passing score and the highest and lowest acceptable pass rate.

These judgments, combined with the test score data, lead to a cutscore for each individual participant.

Advantages and Disadvantages of the Beuk and Hofstee Methods

The major advantage of these methods is that they combine explicit consideration of pass rates with the judgments that produce the cutscore. The Beuk method is reasonably simple and provides a rationale for deciding how much weight to give to the absolute judgments (cutscores) and to the relative judgments (passing rates).

One problem that can occur with the Hofstee method is that there may be no cutscore within the acceptable range that will produce a pass rate within the acceptable range. However, a possible advantage of the Hofstee method is that, unlike the Beuk method, it can be used to compute a separate cutscore for each participant, as well as for the combined judgments of the group.

---

[22] Another compromise method, that of de Gruijter, is based on essentially the same logic as Beuk's method, but uses a more complicated mathematical formula.

5. HOW TO CHOOSE A METHOD

If you already know which method you are going to use, you can skip all of section 5. If you have already narrowed down your choices of a method to a few possibilities, you can skip section 5.1. If, however, you need some help in deciding which methods are most appropriate for your circumstances, read all of section 5.

5.1 Find Appropriate Methods

Each method of setting cutscores has certain requirements, and you cannot use a method unless you can meet its requirements. For example, the Bookmark method requires test questions that have been calibrated using Item Response Theory. If the questions have not been calibrated using IRT, the Bookmark method will not be appropriate for your circumstances.

> *Each method of setting cutscores has certain requirements, and you cannot use a method unless you can meet its requirements.*

You can find appropriate methods for your circumstances by using the following list of methods and the questions that appear below it. First, answer the questions. Then use your answers to shorten the list of methods by eliminating the methods for which you lack the prerequisites. When you finish answering all of the questions, you can choose your method from among those remaining on the list, all of which should be appropriate for you. We provide some recommendations to help you choose the most appropriate method from among those available to you.

Here is the list of methods that we presented:

Methods Based on Judgments of Test Questions

- Angoff method
- Angoff Mean Estimation method
- Angoff Yes or No method
- Nedelsky method
- Ebel method
- Bookmark method
- Item Descriptor Matching method

Methods Based on Judgments of Profiles
- Performance Profile method
- Dominant Profile method

Methods Based on Judgments of People or Products
- Borderline Group method
- Contrasting Groups method
- Up and Down Modification of the Contrasting Groups method
- Body of Work method
- Analytic Judgment method

Methods Based on Judgments of Groups
- Single Reference Group method
- Two Reference Groups method

Compromise Methods
- Beuk method
- Hofstee method

The following questions will help you find the methods of setting cutscores that are appropriate for your circumstances.

1. Can you get a substantial number of people like the intended test takers to take the test, in time to use their responses for choosing the cutscore?
   - If NO, eliminate the Performance Profile method, and all of the methods based on judgments of people or products, methods based on judgments of groups, and the compromise methods.

2. Can you have the test questions calibrated using Item Response Theory before you have to hold the cutscore study?
   - If NO, eliminate the Bookmark and Item Descriptor Matching methods.

3. Are subscores on parts of the test meaningful and useful in evaluating test taker performance?
   - If NO, eliminate the methods based on judgments of profiles.

4. Does the test consist mostly or entirely of constructed-response or performance questions?

   - If NO, eliminate the Performance Profile, Body of Work and Analytic Judgment methods.

5. Does the test consist entirely of multiple-choice questions?

   - If NO, eliminate the Nedelsky method.

6. Do the test questions vary greatly in importance or relevance for what the test is supposed to be measuring?

   - If NO, eliminate the Ebel method

7. Will security considerations allow the participants in the cutscore study to see test questions?

   - If NO, eliminate the methods based on judgments of test questions. Because it is difficult to evaluate responses without seeing the questions, you may wish to eliminate the Performance Profile, Analytic Judgment and Body of Work methods as well.

8. Can you obtain valid judgments about the qualifications of a group of test takers whose test score distribution you can obtain?

   - If NO, eliminate methods based on judgments about groups.

See section 5.2 to help you choose among the methods that are appropriate for your circumstances. If you have eliminated all of the methods, you will not be able to use any of the methods described in this manual, unless you can find a way to change your answers to one or more of the questions.

5.2 Which Method Should You Use?

There is no single correct answer to the question of which method to use. The choice of a cutscore method requires that you weigh many variables such as availability of qualified participants, availability of data, availability of competent facilitators, cost, time required, political acceptability,

> *There is no single correct answer to the question of which method to use.*

90

vulnerability to legal challenge, convenience, amount of available research, compatibility with previously used methods, personal preferences, and so forth. Equally competent people will assign different weights to different variables and arrive at different choices. The advice that follows is based on our combined judgments, but we do not always agree with each other about the preferred cutscore method in a particular situation. We do agree that the best kinds of data to use in a cutscore study, if you can get them, are the test scores of real test takers whose performance has been meaningfully judged by qualified participants.

> *...the best kinds of data to use in a cutscore study ... are the test scores of real test takers whose performance has been meaningfully judged by qualified participants.*

If you can have the participants actually observe the test takers' performance or samples of their work, we recommend the Contrasting Groups method, the Body of Work method, or the Analytic Judgment method. This situation will occur fairly often with essay tests, performance tests, and the like.

The Contrasting Groups method is the most general of the three and can be used with long or short-term evaluations of test takers, or with evaluations of products made by the test takers, including responses to constructed-response and performance questions. The Analytic Judgment and Body of Work methods are limited to tests consisting of mostly performance and constructed-response questions. If you think that judgments of the responses to individual questions are more meaningful than judgments of the test takers' work on the test as a whole, use the Analytic Judgment method. If you believe that judgments of the test taker's work on the test as a whole are more meaningful than the judgments of responses to individual test questions, use the Body of Work method.

For multiple-choice tests, we recommend using the Contrasting Groups method whenever you can be reasonably sure that the participants can and will base their judgments of the test takers on the knowledge and skills that the test is intended to measure.

The Contrasting Groups method has the strongest theoretical rationale of any of the methods we have presented: that of statistical decision theory. It enables you to estimate the frequencies of the two types of misclassifications. The main disadvantage of the Contrasting Groups method is the difficulty of getting the necessary judgments for a large sample of test takers, especially for tests that measure knowledge and skills that are difficult to observe.

For the Contrasting Groups method, the sample of test takers *at each score level* has to be representative of the population of test takers at that score level. If you cannot get good judgments of an appropriate sample of the test takers for the Contrasting Groups method, but each participant can confidently identify individual test takers as good examples of people with borderline qualifications, we recommend the Borderline Group method. If the participants can best express their standards in terms of the performance of a particular group of test takers, we recommend using the Single Reference Group method.[23]

If none of these conditions can be met, you will have to use one of the methods based on judgments about test questions or profiles. If you use such methods, we strongly recommend that you obtain real question and test score data from real test takers to provide to the participants. In the absence of these kinds of data, the cutscores based on judgments of test questions may be unrealistic.

> **Consider methods based on judgments of profiles when there is important information contained in the subscores that is not present in the total score.**

Consider methods based on judgments of profiles when there is important information contained in the subscores that is not present in the total score. Also, consider methods based on judgments of profiles if high performance on some subscores should not be allowed to compensate for low performance on other subscores.

The methods based on judgments of test questions obviously require the participants to see the test questions. If security

---

[23] The Two Reference Groups method is best suited for obtaining a rough estimate of where in the score scale the cutscore is likely to be, or for corroborating the results of a method based on judgments of test questions.

considerations prevent you from showing the test to the participants before the test is administered, you may be able to wait and run the cutscore study after the test has been given. If you do not have this option, you may be able to collect the participants' judgments and set the cutscore on another form of the test (containing different questions measuring the same abilities). This approach will work only if scores on the form to be judged will be statistically equated to scores on the form you will be administering to test takers. Statistical equating makes the scores on the two forms comparable, so that cutscores set for one form can be applied to scores on the other. If none of these options is open to you, you will not be able to use a method based on judgments of test questions.

Consider methods based on judgments of test questions if it is very important to have the cutscores represent the judgments of a large and diverse group of people in a relatively public process. For example, in choosing the passing score on a math test used as a requirement for high school graduation, it may

> *Consider methods based on judgments of test questions if it is very important to have the cutscores represent the judgments of a large and diverse group of people in a relatively public process.*

be important to include the opinions of parents, policymakers, potential employers, college admissions officers, and community leaders. These people are not in a position to observe the mathematical skills of high school students, so they cannot serve as participants in the Borderline Group or Contrasting Groups methods based on judgments of people. But they can serve as participants in methods based on judgments of test questions.

The question-judgment methods have been widely used and some of them have been the subject of a great deal of research. Lawyers for jurisdictions setting cutscores are more comfortable with commonly used methods than with less popular methods. In effect, the methods are popular now in part because they have been popular in the past.

By far, the most widely used methods based on judgments of test questions are the Angoff and Bookmark methods. To date, there is far more research available on the Angoff method than on the Bookmark method. In K–12 state accountability testing, however, the Bookmark method is now used by more states than is the Angoff method. In occupational testing, the Angoff method is more widely used than is the Bookmark method.

The Bookmark method depends on the order of difficulty of the test questions, but the difficulties of questions in new testing programs (completely new programs, not new forms of existing tests) are likely to change rapidly as people become familiar with the content covered by the test. Curricula and training programs are usually changed to cover the knowledge and skills measured by a new test. As a result, some of the questions that are difficult the first year may become easy the next year, thereby changing the order of the questions by difficulty on which the Bookmark cutscore depends.

Between the Bookmark and Item Descriptor Matching methods, the Bookmark method has the advantage of being much more widely used than the Item Descriptor Matching method. But the Item Descriptor Matching method has the advantage of not relying on the concept of a hypothetical test taker answering a question with a specific response probability. Therefore, the participant's task is easier for the Item Descriptor Matching method. Both methods are equally difficult in terms of material preparation, but the Item Descriptor Matching method requires more data entry. See section 6, *Detailed Procedures*, for a way to combine aspects of the Bookmark and ID Matching methods.

Among the question judgment methods, the Ebel method is particularly useful if the test questions differ widely in importance or relevance to what the test is supposed to measure. Such differences can occur, for example, if a test is used in several different states with different curricula.[24] The Nedelsky method is useful when the answer choices in a multiple-choice test describe actions to be taken, and those actions clearly differ in their real world consequences, as may be the case in medical or other occupational tests. The method is also useful if the wrong answers were constructed to reflect specific incorrect procedures or types of misinformation.

---

[24] If the Ebel method identifies many questions of low relevance, we suggest taking steps to improve the test.

Of the two compromise methods we discussed, we prefer Beuk's method. The calculations are not too complex, and we think it makes sense to give each type of judgment (cutscore or pass rate) a weight that depends on the extent to which the participants agree with each other.

6. DETAILED PROCEDURES FOR SETTING CUTSCORES

This section contains the detailed procedures for conducting cutscore studies for the methods we described in section 4. We suggest that you read the overviews of the methods in section 4 and then choose the methods that are most appropriate for your circumstances by using the information in section 5. Read the detailed procedures for the methods of interest to you.

The procedures for a method will not be meaningful unless you have first read the overview of the method in section 4. Remember that you must take the steps described in section 3 before you use any of the procedures detailed in this section to conduct a cutscore study. Please see section 7.1 for evaluative questions to keep in mind as you conduct a cutscore study.

6.1 Procedures for the Angoff Method

Before participants make any judgments about test questions, be sure the participants understand the performance level descriptors and the meaning of borderline performance for each performance level. The participants should also be familiar with the test questions.

> *Before participants make any judgments about test questions, be sure the participants understand the performance level descriptors and the meaning of borderline performance for each performance level.*

1. Have the participants make preliminary judgments for the first few questions. Each judgment is the participant's estimate of the probability that a borderline test taker would answer the question correctly.

The judgments may be difficult for some participants. If the participants are not comfortable making judgments in terms of probabilities, ask them to imagine a group of 100 borderline test takers and decide how many of them would answer the question correctly. Obviously, the easier the question, the higher this number will be.

The probability that a borderline test taker will answer a multiple-choice question correctly must be between 0.00 and 1.00. The number out of 100 borderline test takers who will answer a multiple-choice question correctly must be between 0 and 100. When you enter the data to calculate the cutscore, be sure to write the numbers as decimal numbers (e.g., 25 should be entered as .25).

If the questions are multiple choice, the probability of a correct answer should ordinarily be at least as large as the chance of guessing the correct answer by pure luck (that is, 1.00 divided by the number of choices). For example, explain to participants that a test taker who guesses on a four-choice question has a .25 probability of guessing correctly. Their rating for that question should not fall below 0.25 unless they believe there is an incorrect answer that would be particularly appealing to borderline test takers. Some facilitators say that the highest probability should be 0.95 because even people who have mastered a particular skill may make occasional mistakes. If you share this belief and you want to communicate it to the participants, be sure to tell them that it is simply your belief. Do not try to substitute your judgment for their judgments about the test questions.

2. Conduct a brief discussion of each of the test questions.

Have each participant report his or her choice of a probability for each question. Display these numbers on a screen or write them on a white board or a large sheet of paper so all the participants can see them. If the numbers are all similar (e.g., within 10 or so percentage points), go on to the next question.

If the numbers are not all similar, ask for a participant who chose one of the highest numbers to explain the reasons for choosing a high probability. Then ask for a participant who chose one of the lowest numbers to explain the reasons for choosing a low probability. Encourage discussion among the participants. Tell the participants they can change their judgments if they want to. Make sure the participants understand that their judgments are supposed to describe the performance of *borderline* test takers.

3. After discussing the first few questions, have the participants make preliminary judgments for the remaining questions on their own.

4. Collect and record the judgments and prepare summary feedback data such as the participants' estimates for each test question and for the overall cutscore arrived at by summing each participant's probability estimates.

5. Discuss the remaining questions as in step 2, and give the participants a chance to change their judgments if they want to.

   In some cases, when you are working with a large number of test questions and have limited time, you may want to select a subset of the questions for discussion. That is, instead of asking the participants to discuss all 100 test questions, you may select for discussion only the 30 questions on which the participants disagreed most strongly. Encourage the participants to feel free to discuss any other questions they wish.

6. Collect and record the judgments.

7. We suggest that you have two or three iterations of judgments and provide information to the participants between the iterations. For example, if you choose to have three iterations, you could provide information about the difficulty of the questions and the cutscores selected by other participants after the first round of judgments, and about the consequences of using the interim cutscores after the second round of judgments.

8. Calculate the cutscore.

   If a test taker receives one point for a correct answer and no points for any other response (or for omitting the question), the test taker's expected score for any question is equal to the probability of choosing the correct answer. Simply add the probabilities for the individual questions to get the borderline test taker's expected score for the whole test. Do this computation separately for each individual participant.[25] See Figure 3 for an example of the calculations. You can combine the scores you have computed for the individual participants by computing the mean, or the median, or the trimmed mean.

---

[25] If the test is scored with a correction for guessing, you will have to subtract the expected number of correct answers from the number of questions to get the expected number of wrong answers. Then multiply this number by the penalty for each wrong answer, and subtract that number from the expected number of correct answers to get the participant's estimate of the test taker's expected score.

98

Figure 3. Example of Calculations for the Angoff Method for
One Participant on a Ten Question Test

Question	Probability of Correct Answer
1	.95
2	.80
3	.90
4	.60
5	.75
6	.40
7	.50
8	.25
9	.25
10	.40
	Sum = 5.80

6.2 Procedures for the Angoff Mean Estimation Method

Give the participants the scoring rubrics that have been
developed for the essay or performance questions. The rubrics
describe the important characteristics of a response at each
score level. Also, give the participants sample responses at
each score level to help the participants understand the
knowledge and skills required to reach each score level.

Follow the procedures listed above for the Angoff method with
one exception. Instead of asking participants to estimate the
probability of a correct response on a multiple-choice question,
ask the participants to estimate the average score that borderline
test takers would get on an essay or performance question.

6.3 Procedures for the Angoff Yes or No Method

Follow the procedures listed above for the Angoff method with
one exception. Instead of asking participants to estimate the
probability of a correct response, ask the participants to decide
whether or not the borderline test taker would answer the
question correctly.

Tell the participants to write *yes* for questions the borderline test
taker would answer correctly, and *no* for the questions the
borderline test taker would not answer correctly. The cutscore

for a participant is simply the number of questions for which the participant's answer was *yes*.

If the test consists of multiple-choice questions scored without a correction for guessing, we recommend a variation of the Yes or No method. On these questions, the expected score for a test taker who does not know the answer is not zero; it is the probability of answering the question correctly by guessing. That probability is 1 divided by the number of answers the test taker has to choose from. On a four-choice question, that probability is 1 in 4, or .25. On a five-choice question, it is 1 in 5, or .20. We suggest that you sum these probabilities for the questions for which the participant's answer was *no*. Then add that sum to the number of questions for which the participant's answer was *yes*, to get the recommended cutscore for the participant.

We realize that test takers who do not know the answer to a question often do not guess at random. Sometimes they are drawn to a specific wrong answer; sometimes they eliminate one or more wrong answers before guessing among the remaining choices. On the whole, however, we think that using the random-guessing probability as the expected score is much better than assuming that the possibility of guessing correctly is zero.

6.4 Procedures for the Nedelsky Method

Before participants make any judgments about test questions, be sure the participants understand the performance level descriptors, and the meaning of borderline performance for each performance level. The participants should also be familiar with the test questions.

Negatively worded questions can present a problem in using the Nedelsky method. An even greater problem is caused by questions in a two-stage format (sometimes called "multiple true-false"), e.g. "Choose A if only statement I is true; Choose B if only statements I and III are true; etc." If your test has such questions, give the participants plenty of practice at judging those kinds of questions before they begin making their operational judgments. Ask the participants to explain the reasons for their judgments on at least some of those questions, to make sure their selections of answers to be eliminated are what they really intended.

Another type of question that can present difficulties in using the Nedelsky method is the question that requires the test taker to do some mathematical computation. The wrong answer choices to these questions usually are the results of common mistakes. The difficulties arise because the type of mistake that a wrong answer choice indicates is not always obvious. Therefore, the participants may have a hard time deciding whether or not a borderline test taker would have selected a particular wrong answer. Even the most qualified participants may find it time-consuming to figure out what kind of mistake would lead to each wrong answer. You can avoid this problem and save time by giving the participants a copy of the test on which you have indicated the types of mistakes that lead to each wrong answer choice.

Here are the procedures for the Nedelsky method.

1. Have the participants make a set of preliminary judgments for all the questions.

   Have the participants work individually and use a pencil to mark the wrong answers the borderline test taker would be able to eliminate.

2. Conduct a brief discussion of each question.

   Focus the participants' attention on the first wrong answer. Ask how many of them thought the borderline test taker would be able to eliminate it as incorrect (i.e., not the best answer), and how many did not think so.

   If the participants are not unanimous, ask one participant who marked the answer to explain why. Then ask one participant who did not mark that answer to explain why not. Do not try to reach agreement; just allow each point of view to be heard. Encourage discussion among the participants. The participants may or may not be swayed by the comments of their colleagues. Tell the participants they may change their judgments if they want to. Make sure the participants understand that their judgments are supposed to describe the performance of a *borderline* test taker. Go on to the next wrong answer.

3. After all the questions have been discussed in this manner, ask the participants to review their decisions and make sure they have marked *all* the wrong answers they intended to mark and *only* those answers.

4. Collect the judgments.

   To save time, you can use a shortcut version of this technique in which you consider each question as a whole:

   a. Ask how many participants eliminated all the wrong answers.

   b. Ask how many participants eliminated the first wrong answer, how many eliminated the second wrong answer, and so on.

   c. Ask one of the participants to explain his or her reasoning in deciding which wrong answers to eliminate.

   d. Ask one of the participants who made a different decision to explain his or her reasoning.

   e. Allow discussion as long as the discussion seems to be productive. Then remind the participants that they can change their judgments if they want to.

   f. Go on to the next question. You may find it useful to begin by discussing each wrong answer and then switch, after a few questions, to discussing the question as a whole.

5. We suggest that you have two or three rounds of judgments and provide information to the participants between the rounds. For example, if you choose to have three rounds of judgments, provide information about the difficulty of the questions and the cutscores selected by other participants after the first round, and about the consequences of using the interim cutscores after the second round. You may also wish to provide information about the proportion of test takers who chose each incorrect answer.

6. Calculate the cutscore.

   The Nedelsky method is based on the idea that the borderline test taker who does not know the answer to a multiple-choice question will eliminate the answers he or she recognizes as wrong and then choose one of the others, with the same probability of choosing the correct answer as if he or she were choosing at random from the answers not eliminated. It is relatively easy to find the score that such a test taker would be expected to get, by applying the following rules:

The test taker's expected score for any question is 1 divided by the number of choices the test taker has to guess from, as shown in Figure 4.

Figure 4. Test Taker's Expected Score for a Question

Number of Choices Remaining (Right Answer Plus Any Remaining Wrong Answers)	Probability of a Correct Response
1	1/1 = 1.00
2	1/2 = 0.50
3	1/3 = 0.33
4	1/4 = 0.25
5	1/5 = 0.20

To find a participant's estimate of a borderline test taker's expected score for the whole test, add up that test taker's expected scores for all the individual questions. Combine the cutscores across participants using the mean, trimmed mean, or median as the group cutscore.

6.5 Procedures for the Ebel Method

Before participants make any judgments about test questions, be sure the participants understand the performance level descriptors, and the meaning of borderline performance for each performance level. The participants should also be familiar with the test questions.

The group procedure for judgments and discussion that we recommend for the Nedelsky and Angoff methods can be adapted for the Ebel method. However, it will be more complicated, because the participants must make two decisions about each individual test question: its difficulty (if no data are available) and its relevance. Participants must then make a judgment about the borderline test taker's performance on each group of questions.

The procedure consists of the following steps.

1. The participant's first task is to classify all the questions in the test by difficulty. If you have statistics indicating the

difficulty of each question, you can substitute your data for the participant's judgments.[26]

Have the participants make a preliminary classification of the test questions into the categories of difficulty and importance, working individually.

2. Conduct a brief discussion of each question.

If there are no data, ask how many participants classified the question as "easy," as "medium," and as "hard." If the participants were not unanimous, ask one participant who classified the question as "easy" to explain why. Do the same for "medium" and "hard." Encourage discussion among the participants.

3. The participant's next step is to classify all of the questions by relevance or importance.

Ask how many participants classified the question as "essential," as "important," as "acceptable," and as "questionable." If the participants are not unanimous, ask one participant who chose each category to explain why. Encourage discussion among the participants and give the participants a chance to reclassify the question if they want to.

4. The participant's next task is to make a judgment about the performance of a borderline test taker on each of the groups of questions created by classifying the questions by difficulty and relevance/importance. The participant must make one judgment for the questions classified "essential, easy," another for the questions classified "essential, medium," and so on, all the way down to "questionable, hard."

Have the participants make a preliminary judgment, for each group of questions, of the percentage of such questions a borderline test taker would answer correctly. Ask the participants to answer the question: "If a borderline test taker had to answer a large number of questions like these, what percentage of them would he or she answer correctly?" See Figure 5 for an example of Steps 3 and 4.

---

[26] This recommendation is based on our assumption that question difficulty for all test takers is highly correlated with question difficulty for borderline test takers.

Figure 5. Example of Classification of Questions and Judgments in the Ebel Method

	Easy	Medium	Hard
Relevance			
Essential	Questions: 1, 4, 7, 8, 13 Judgment: 95%	Questions: 11, 15, 22 Judgment: 85%	Question: 21 Judgment: 80%
Important	Questions: 2, 6, 9 Judgment: 90%	Questions: 10, 14, 20 Judgment: 75%	Questions: 16, 25 Judgment: 60%
Acceptable	Question: 5 Judgment: 80%	Questions: 12, 18 Judgment: 55%	Questions: 19, 23 Judgment: 35%
Questionable	Question: 3 Judgment: 50%	Question: None	Questions 17, 24 Judgment: 20%

5. Conduct a brief discussion for each group of questions.

   Point out that one of the possible reasons for differences in the participants' percentages is that participants may have placed some different questions in the category. If the participants have differed greatly in their placement of questions into categories, further discussion of their judgments about the percentage of questions in a category that a borderline test taker would answer correctly may not be fruitful.

   If, however, there tends to be general agreement about the questions placed in each category, have each participant announce his or her choice of a percentage for that category. Ask a participant who chose one of the highest numbers to explain the reasons for choosing a high percentage. Then ask a participant who chose one of the lowest numbers to explain the reasons for choosing a low percentage. Encourage discussion among the participants of the questions in each category and the percentages that they selected.

   Tell the participants they may change their judgments if they want to. Make sure the participants understand that the judgments are supposed to describe the performance of a *borderline* test taker.

6. Collect the judgments.

   We suggest that you have two or three iterations of judgments and provide information to the participants between the iterations. For example, if you have three rounds of judgments, you could provide information about the cutscores selected by other participants after the first round of judgments, and about the consequences of using the interim cutscores after the second round of judgments.

7. Calculate the cutscore.

   To find the participant's expected test score for a borderline test taker, use the following procedure:

   (1) Multiply the judged percentage correct (expressed as a decimal number) for each group of questions (e.g., "essential, easy") by the number of questions in that group to get the test taker's expected score for that group of questions.

   (2) Add the expected scores for all of the groups of questions to get the participant's expected score for the whole test. See Figure 6 on the next page for an example of the calculations.

You can combine the scores you have computed for the individual participants in the same way as for the Nedelsky or Angoff methods, by computing the mean, the median, or the trimmed mean.

6.6 Procedures for the Bookmark Method

Before participants make any judgments about test questions, be sure the participants understand the performance level descriptors, and the meaning of borderline performance for each performance level. The participants should also be familiar with the test questions.

Steps 1 and 2 (Produce an Ordered Item Booklet and Produce an Item Map) must be completed before the cutscore study begins. It can be a time-consuming task to produce the Ordered Item Booklet and the Item Map, so be sure to begin your preparations well in advance of the meeting.

Figure 6. Example of Calculations for the Ebel Method

Category	Judgment of Percent Correct	Number of Questions in Category	Expected Score for Category
Essential			
Easy	95	5	.95 X 5 = 4.75
Medium	85	3	.85 X 3 = 2.55
Hard	80	1	.80 X 1 = 0.80
Important			
Easy	90	3	.90 X 3 = 2.70
Medium	75	3	.75 X 3 = 2.25
Hard	60	2	.60 X 2 = 1.20
Acceptable			
Easy	80	1	.80 X 1 = 0.80
Medium	55	2	.55 X 2 = 1.10
Hard	35	2	.35 X 2 = 0.70
Questionable			
Easy	50	1	.50 X 1 = 0.50
Medium		0	0
Hard	20	2	.20 X 2 = 0.40
			Expected Total Score = Sum = 17.75

1. Produce an Ordered Item Booklet in which the test questions are arranged from easy to hard in order of their IRT difficulty values.[27]

   Start each question on a separate page of the Ordered Item Booklet. All of the information for a question may take more than one page in the Ordered Item Booklet. There should never be more than one test question on a page of the Ordered Item Booklet.

---

[27] Unless the questions were calibrated using a one-parameter IRT model, tell the statistician you are working with that the questions should be ordered based on their difficulty at a Response Probability of .67.

If the test includes constructed-response questions such as essay questions, make separate sets of pages for each possible score on the question except the score of 0.[28] For example, if the question has possible scores of 0, 1, 2, and 3, make three separate sets of pages for that question: one set of pages for a score of 1 on the question, another set of pages for a score of 2, and another set of pages for a score of 3. The page(s) for a score of 1 should contain the question, the scoring rule ("rubric") for a score of 1 and a typical response that received a score of 1. The page(s) for a score of 2 should contain the question, the scoring rule ("rubric") for a score of 2 and a typical response that received a score of 2, and similarly for the page(s) for a score of 3.

> *It can be a time-consuming task to produce the Ordered Item Booklet and the Item Map, so be sure to begin your preparations well in advance of the meeting.*

Each of the sets of pages for the different scores on the same constructed-response question will appear at a different place in the Ordered Item Booklet. This will happen because the questions are arranged in order of difficulty, and higher scores on constructed-response questions are more difficult to obtain than are lower scores. For example, it is easy to get a score of 1, harder to get a score of 2, and still harder to get a score of 3. It is unlikely that these sets of pages will be next to each other. Other questions are likely to come in between the different appearances of a constructed-response question in the Ordered Item Booklet.

In the Ordered Item Booklet, number each appearance of the same constructed-response question with a different score. Use a decimal number. Put the original question number before the decimal and the score after the decimal. For example, question 18 in the original test book (not the Ordered Item Booklet) with a score of 1 is numbered as question 18.1, question 18 with a score of 2 is numbered as question 18.2, and so forth. Question 18.1 may be in

---

[28] We assume that the essay question, the scoring rubric and a sample response will require several pages.

difficulty order 25 in the Ordered Item Booklet. Question 18.2 may be in difficulty order 36 in the Ordered Item Booklet, and so forth.

Because you may need several pages in the Ordered Item Booklet to display all of the information for one question, we recommend numbering both the pages and the questions. For example, an Ordered Item Booklet may have question 36 on page 54, so be sure that it is clear which number applies to the page and which number applies to the question. One possibility is to number the questions Q1, Q2, Q3 and so forth, and to number the pages P1, P2, P3, and so forth.

2. Next, produce an Item Map like the one shown in Figure 7. The Item Map is a table or chart that shows for each question:

   - its number in the Ordered Item Booklet,
   - its original question number in the test booklet (i.e., the order in which it appeared when the test taker took the test),
   - the correct answer (for multiple-choice questions) or point value (for constructed-response questions)
   - its difficulty, and
   - the knowledge and skills, content standard, objective, or specification that the question is supposed to measure.

The Item Map lists the questions in the same order as they are in the Ordered Item Booklet.

Figure 7 shows a typical Item Map. The first column displays the ordered item number that corresponds to the location of the question in the Ordered Item Booklet. The second column indicates the original question number on the test. Note that for constructed-response questions, the score of the response to the question is indicated in this column along with the original question number. For instance, ordered question 5 corresponds to the location associated with the difficulty of receiving 1 point on original question 16 (16.1). Ordered question 12 is the location associated with the difficulty of receiving 2 points on original question 16 (16.2), and ordered question 19 is the location associated with the difficulty of receiving 3 points on this same question (16.3).

Figure 7. Illustrative Item Map for a Mathematics Test

Item Difficulty Order (easiest to most difficult)	Original Item No.	Answer key	Item difficulty	Content Strand	Comments
1	9	A	450	Data, Statistics, and Probability	
2	19	C	454	Number Systems	
3	24	D	460	Measurement	
4	13	A	465	Geometry	
5	16.1	?	470	Measurement	
6	27	B	472	Patterns, Algebra, and Functions	
7	20	B	475	Number Systems	
8	10	B	479	Number Systems	
9	25.1	?	480	Patterns, Algebra, and Functions	
10	2	C	482	Number Systems	
11	21	D	485	Data, Statistics, and Probability	
12	16.2	?	488	Measurement	
13	5	A	490	Measurement	
14	4	D	494	Number Systems	
15	6.1	?	499	Patterns, Algebra, and Functions	
16	15.1	?	500	Measurement	
17	14	B	502	Geometry	
18	8	A	502	Number Systems	
19	16.3	?	504	Measurement	
20	25.2	?	505	Patterns, Algebra, and Functions	
21	1	A	506	Patterns, Algebra, and Functions	

Figure 7. Illustrative Item Map for a Mathematics Test (Continued)

Item Difficulty Order (easiest to most difficult)	Original Item No.	Answer key	Item difficulty	Content Strand	Comments
22	23	C	507	Number Systems	
23	26.1	~	508	Geometry	
24	30	B	509	Number Systems	
25	7	D	511	Data, Statistics, and Probability	
26	6.2	~	512	Patterns, Algebra, and Functions	
27	15.2	~	513	Measurement	
28	3	D	515	Patterns, Algebra, and Functions	
29	18	A	515	Measurement	
30	11	D	516	Number Systems	
31	26.2	~	517	Geometry	
32	22	B	519	Patterns, Algebra, and Functions	
33	29	C	521	Geometry	
34	12	C	522	Patterns, Algebra, and Functions	
35	6.3	~	524	Patterns, Algebra, and Functions	
36	28	A	525	Geometry	
37	17	D	527	Geometry	
38	12	C	529	Patterns, Algebra, and Functions	

The next two columns show the correct answer to the question and the question's difficulty. The difficulty can be the IRT scale location at a response probability of .67. It also can be a simple linear transformation of the IRT difficulty parameter. The purpose of this column is to indicate the relative difficulty of one question compared to another. The next column indicates the content strand measured by the question, and the last column (typically wider in an operational Item Map) provides space for the participant to jot down any notes or observations about the question.

3. Appoint a Table Leader from among the participants for each table (see #4). The job of the Table Leader is to keep the participants at his or her table on task, to keep the participants working at an appropriate pace, and to report the results of the work done at the table to the total group of participants.

   The Table Leader does not have to be an expert in setting cutscores, but should be comfortable leading small groups. You should provide the Table Leaders additional training on their role. Make sure the Table Leaders know the work that is to be done at the tables and how much time is to be allotted to each task. Also make the Table Leaders aware of when they will be called on to report the results of the judgments made at their tables to the whole group of participants, and how much time will be allotted for each report.

4. Seat the participants in small groups at separate tables.

   Much of the discussion at a Bookmark session takes place among participants seated at the same table. Participants are usually seated in 3–5 tables of 5–8 participants per table. Try for a mix of people at each table that is similar to the mix of people in the whole group. For example, if you have both teachers and administrators among the participants, try to include some teachers and some administrators at each table. To ensure an appropriate mix of people at each table, it is best to assign participants to tables rather than allowing them to choose where to sit.

5. Give participants the Item Map and the Ordered Item Booklet. Explain the documents.

Emphasize that the questions in the Ordered Item Booklet are in order from easy to hard. Also point out that the questions on adjacent pages could be very similar in difficulty, or they could be very different in difficulty. For example, the seventh question in difficulty order may be just slightly harder than the sixth question in difficulty order, but the eighth question in difficulty order may be substantially harder than the seventh question. Explain how the participants can use the Item Map to determine the difficulties of the test questions. Ask the participants to read through the Ordered Item Booklet page by page. As they read each page of the Ordered Item Booklet, they should refer to the corresponding part of the Item Map and discuss their answers to the following questions:

- What does a test taker have to know and be able to do to answer this test question correctly (or to earn the number of points indicated, if the question is a constructed-response question)?

- What are the aspects of this question that make it more difficult than the questions appearing before it in the Ordered Item Booklet?

This task helps participants focus on the match between the knowledge and skills required to answer each question and the knowledge and skills of the borderline test taker. You should typically allot at least one minute per test question for this activity. Tell the participants not to discuss bookmark placements at this point but to work together to ensure they have a common understanding of the cognitive requirements of each question.

Questions may sometimes appear "out of order" to the participants. For example, a question that appears easy to the participants may have been difficult for test takers because it was placed near the end of the test booklet. Some test takers may have been fatigued by the time they reached the question and possibly did not consider the question carefully. Participants often ask, "Why did you order the questions this way?" Make clear to the participants that the order of the questions in the Ordered Item Booklet is based on a statistical analysis of the responses of real test takers. Remind the participants that in some parts of the Ordered Item Booklet adjacent questions may be very nearly equal in difficulty, while in other parts of the booklet the differences in difficulty between adjacent questions may be much greater. Also, remind participants that the Item Map shows the actual, not judged, difficulties of the test questions.

6. Ask participants to read through the Ordered Item Booklet from the easiest question to the hardest question and to place a "bookmark" at the point between the last question that borderline test takers would probably answer correctly and the first question that borderline test takers would probably not be able to answer correctly.[29] For any page that indicates a score on a constructed-response question, substitute "would probably earn at least that score" for "would probably answer correctly."

The word "probably" is typically defined for this purpose as a probability of at least two-thirds, 2 out of 3, or .67. This probability is also called a *Response Probability* of .67 or RP67.[30] For constructed-response questions, tell participants to determine whether or not a borderline test taker would be able to get at least that number of points on questions similar to this question two-thirds of the time.

Alternatively, you could tell participants to determine whether or not two-thirds of a large group of borderline test takers would be able to get at least that number of points on this question. Instruct the participants not to consider guessing on multiple choice questions. Tell the participants to focus on the proportion of borderline test takers who would know (not guess) the answer to the question.

---

[29] Some facilitators tell the participants to place the bookmark *on* the first question that borderline test takers would probably not be able to answer correctly. Conceptually, the bookmark is placed *between* two questions. Physically, the bookmark is usually a sticky piece of paper that is placed *on* a question. For example, if the bookmark belongs *between* questions 17 and 18, it may be placed *on* question 18.

[30] Response probabilities other than .67, such as .50 and .80 have been used, but .67 is the most commonly used response probability for Bookmark studies.

114

In our experience, the RP67 is a difficult concept for
participants. We do not think participants can distinguish
between a response probability of .67 and a response
probability of .65 or .70. Rather than focusing on fine
distinctions among probabilities, try alternative wording such
as "The borderline test taker is twice as likely to get
questions like this one right as she is to get them wrong. The
borderline test taker would get questions like this one right
two times out of three." You could also try wording such as,
"if the borderline test taker had to answer many questions
just like this one in terms of content and difficulty, would he
or she answer at least two-thirds of them correctly? When
the answer to this question is 'no,' stop and place your
bookmark." For constructed-response questions ask , "if the
borderline test taker had to answer many questions like this
one in terms of content and difficulty, would he or she receive at
least this many points on two thirds of the questions?"

7. After participants place their bookmarks, encourage them to
continue through the booklet looking for more questions that
the borderline test taker would probably answer correctly.
The purpose of continuing the search is to prevent
participants from placing the bookmark at the first seemingly
difficult question without checking to see whether or not that
question is followed by several apparently easier questions.

Participants may find a few questions after the bookmark
that they think the borderline test taker would be likely to
answer correctly. Ask the participants to look at the two
groups of questions separated by the bookmark to be sure
that the questions before the bookmark are generally questions
that a borderline test taker probably would answer correctly
at least two-thirds of the time and that questions after the
bookmark are generally questions that the borderline test taker
would probably not answer correctly two-thirds of the time.

Some participants in a Bookmark study may stop at the first
question that they believe a borderline test taker will not be
able to answer correctly two-thirds of the time and not go any
further into the test booklet, regardless of the instructions.
Other participants, with exactly the same ideas as to which
questions a borderline test taker would and would not
answer correctly, may temporarily put a bookmark at that
point but continue to review questions, finding a better point
to place their bookmark.

To provide a concrete example, let's consider the judgments that two participants would make about 20 questions in an Ordered Item Booklet. For simplicity's sake, we limit this example to one cutscore. We can show their judgments in a table with a 1 for each question they think a borderline test taker would answer correctly at least two-thirds of the time and a 0 for each question that they think a borderline test taker would not answer correctly at least two-thirds of the time. A slash is used to mark the bookmark locations of the participants.

Question number	1	2	3	4	5	6	7	8	9	10	11	12	13	14	15	16	17	18	19	20
First Participant's Judgments	1	1	1	1	1	1	1	/ 0												
Second Participant's Judgments	1	1	1	1	1	1	1	0	1	1	1	1	/ 0	0	0	0	0	0	0	0

The first participant stops at question 8 and places his bookmark there, without looking at the rest of the questions. The second participant goes further and judges all of the questions. She discovers that there are two possible locations for her bookmark—question 8 and question 13. The table makes clear, however, that question 13 is a more appropriate place for the bookmark.

A useful strategy is to have the participants match each question to the performance level required to respond correctly to the question, as described in steps 3 and 4 of the procedures for the Item Descriptor Matching Method. In this example, B stands for the Basic performance level and P stands for the Proficient performance level.

Question number	1	2	3	4	5	6	7	8	9	10	11	12	13	14	15	16	17	18	19	20
Participant's Judgments	B	B	B	B	B	B	B	P	B	B	B	B	P	P	P	P	P	P	P	P

The completed table makes clear that the appropriate placement for the bookmark is on question 13, not on question 8. Though producing such a table is not typically part of the Bookmark method as it is currently implemented, we recommend having participants complete such a table to avoid premature placement of the bookmark.

In some cases, we have found it helpful to advise a participant to ignore an "out of place" question in the Ordered Item Booklet if that question is causing a problem in placing the bookmark. For example, a participant might say "If question 12 were not here, I would place the bookmark at question 18, but question 12 seems so difficult, I do not think a borderline test taker will be able to answer it correctly." In such a case, encourage the participant to disregard question 12. It is not good to disregard questions, but we think that it is preferable to allowing one or two anomalous questions to determine the placement of the bookmark.

Participants often complain that the test questions that come before the point at which they wish to place their bookmark do not cover all of the content areas that they believe are required for borderline test takers. For example, if the performance level descriptor includes performance in geometry, algebra, measurement, and probability, participants may be concerned if none of the questions before the bookmark is about geometry. To move the bookmark beyond the first geometry question, however, the participants may have to move the bookmark too far into the more difficult questions in the Ordered Item Booklet.

To help alleviate this concern, explain that questions within any content area can be written at many levels of difficulty and that the participants are seeing only one particular test form or one set of questions. It is possible that a different form of the test or different set of questions would have a question on geometry earlier in the Ordered Item Booklet. Remind the participants not to move the bookmark beyond the appropriate difficulty level to include a question that covers a particular content area.

8. If more than one cutscore is being set, tell participants to continue working through the Ordered Item Booklet and to place the remaining bookmark(s) for the next cutscore(s).

9. The Bookmark method generally uses three rounds of judgments. Each round consists of a bookmark placement for each of the cutscores being set (for example, between Basic and Proficient, and between Proficient and Advanced.) After round 1, tell participants how their bookmark placements compared to those of the other participants seated at their table. Typically, the facilitator will provide the

table leader with the placement of the highest, lowest, and median bookmarks at the table and ask the table leader to share the information with the participants at the table. At this point, the participants are not told about the bookmark placements at the other tables.

After the participants receive round 1 feedback, encourage them to discuss their bookmark placements at their tables, starting with the first question that any participant bookmarked and moving sequentially through the questions until they reached the last question any participant bookmarked. Tell participants to focus on the knowledge and skills required to answer correctly each question within that range and to compare the required knowledge and skills to the knowledge and skills of the borderline test taker.

10. After round 2, give participants the range of bookmark placements at their table, and also give them the range of bookmark placements across the entire room. There is typically a whole room discussion at this point with the participants at the different tables sharing the discussions from their table with the others in the room. Ask each table leader to give a 2–3 minute explanation of the discussions that have been occurring at his or her table. These explanations typically focus on test questions that have caused disagreements among the participants.

   Often, the participants at a table are divided between two locations for the bookmark. Discuss these differences with the whole group to see if other tables are having similar problems. After each table leader speaks, give the other participants from that table an opportunity to add to the explanation. Give participants from other tables the opportunity to ask questions. Before moving back into table-level discussions, tell the participants the effects of the round 2 median bookmark cutscores in terms of the percentage of test takers who would fall into each performance level and allow time for a full-room discussion of those data.

11. Have participants place their bookmarks for a third iteration. This is typically the final round of judgments.

12. Calculate the cutscore.

The cutscore recommendation is based on the median bookmark placement. Calculate the median cutscore of each table. Typically the median of the table medians is used as the group's estimate of the cutscore. The median of the whole room could also be taken as the group cutscore, although the median of the table medians is more commonplace.[31]

The location of the group's bookmark is used to identify a point on the difficulty scale.[32] Your statistician can then use IRT to compute the ability of a test taker who would have a .67 probability of correctly answering a question with the difficulty level indicated by the group's bookmark placement. This test taker is the borderline test taker. The IRT analysis can translate the borderline test taker's ability into an expected score on the test. That expected score is the cutscore implied by the process.

13. Review the performance level descriptors (PLDs).

In many Bookmark studies, participants are asked to review the PLDs to make sure they are congruent with the cutpoints that were set at the meeting. We believe that, because the cutscores should have been based on the existing PLDs, it is appropriate to augment and clarify the PLDs at this stage, but not to change them substantially.

6.7 Procedures for the Item Descriptor Matching Method

Before participants make any judgments about test questions, be sure the participants understand the performance level descriptors for each performance level. The participants should also be familiar with the test questions.

---

[31] Usually the results of the two procedures will be very similar, but they can be quite different under certain circumstances.

[32] To identify the best point on the difficulty scale, some people use the average of the difficulties of the questions just before and just after the bookmark. Other people use the difficulty of the question just before the bookmark. We believe the latter tends to bias the cutscore downward.

1. Produce an Ordered Item Booklet and an Item Map as described in the first two steps of the Bookmark method in section 6.6. Step 1 must be completed before the cutscore meeting begins.

2. The discussions required by the Item Descriptor Matching method may be facilitated if the participants are seated in small groups at separate tables. Have the participants go through the Ordered Item Booklet, question by question, and discuss the knowledge and skills required to answer each question correctly (or to achieve the indicated number of points on constructed-response question). For more detail on how to accomplish these actions, read Steps 3-5 of the Bookmark method.

3. Tell the participants, working individually, to match the knowledge and skills required to answer each question to the knowledge and skills described in the performance level descriptors. (You will need a definition of all of the performance levels, including the lowest performance level, for this task.)

   Encourage the participants to read each question, determine what a test taker must know and be able to do to answer that question correctly, and then match the knowledge and skills required to answer the question to the knowledge and skills listed in the performance level descriptors. The goal is to find the one performance level that best matches the knowledge and skill required to answer the question. The participant then writes the initial of the appropriate performance level next to each question on the Item Map or on a separate form.

4. As a participant matches the test questions to the performance level descriptors, the letters indicating performance levels will tend to form a pattern. There will be a sequence of letters indicating the lowest performance level, followed by a sequence in which the letters for that level and the next higher performance level are mixed, followed by a sequence of letters indicating the next higher performance level, and so on. If you are using the performance levels Basic, Proficient, and Advanced, the pattern will tend to look like the following example,

   B B B B B B P B B P P B P P P P P P P P A P A P A A A A A A.

   The *threshold regions* are indicated by underlining in the example shown above. They are defined by the mixed patterns of letters, indicating two different performance levels. The participant's task is to specify a *cutline* in the sequence to separate each pair of adjacent performance levels—the point at which the knowledge and skills required by the test questions are at the borderline between the two levels. In the example above, the participant would specify two cutlines, one to separate Basic from Proficient and one to separate Proficient from Advanced. If no clear pattern of letters emerges for most of the participants, the Item Descriptor Matching method is not working and you will have to set the cutscore by a different method.

5. We suggest that you conduct this process over two or three rounds. After round 1, ask the participants to compare their cutline placements and to discuss those test questions about which they disagreed. Encourage the participants to compare the knowledge and skills required to answer each of these test questions with the knowledge and skills described in the performance level descriptors.

6. In the second round encourage the participants to view the test holistically, rather than one question at a time to ensure that the questions below each cutline generally are matched to the lower level performance level descriptor and the questions above that cutline are generally matched to the next higher level performance level descriptor. Encourage the participants at each table to discuss their differences and try to arrive at cutline placements for the table. It is not a problem if participants at a table do not reach consensus. Share the cutline placements for each table with the total group. If the second round is the final round, go to Step 7 before the second round of judgments are made. If there will be three rounds of judgments, go to Step 7 after the second round.

7. Calculate an interim cutscore as described in Step 8. Before the final round, give participants impact data (the percent of test takers that would fall into each of the performance levels if the current group cutscore were implemented). Hold a room-level discussion about the impact data and the range of cutscore placements. Then allow the participants an opportunity to change their individual cutlines on the basis of the information.

8. Calculate the cutscore.

Each participant has indicated the point between two questions where each cutscore should fall. The point is translated into a cutscore by the same procedure that is used in the Bookmark method. Please see Step 12 of the procedures for the Bookmark method in section 6.6.

If you wish to follow common practice in using the Item Descriptor Matching method, tell your statistician to use a Response Probability of .50 to find the cutscore.[33] The choice of a Response Probability in the Item Descriptor Matching method has no effect on what the participants do and need not be discussed with the participants.

6.8 Procedures for the Performance Profile Method

Before participants make any judgments about test questions, be sure the participants understand the performance level descriptors, and the meaning of borderline performance for each performance level. The participants should also be familiar with the test questions. Complete Steps 1–3 before the cutscore meeting begins.

1. Choose score profiles to be evaluated by the participants.

You need to obtain test takers' score profiles to use this method. Arrange the profiles by total score. Read through the score profiles of test takers with the lowest total score in the range of possible cutscores and choose two to five score profiles that are typical (most frequent) for test takers at that score level. Move up to the next higher total score, review the profiles that summed to that total, and choose two to five profiles that are typical for test takers at that score level. Continue, total score by total score, until you have chosen two to five typical profiles for test takers at the highest score level in the range of possible cutscores. The highest and

---

[33] Several reviewers have asked us to explain why the ID Matching method and the Bookmark method typically use different RP values. We are not sure why and have simply reported common practice for each method. In any case, for the ID Matching method, the participants are never exposed to the concept of the Response Probability.

lowest total scores, for example, are not likely to be in the range of possible cutscores.

2. Make an Ordered Profile Booklet by arranging the chosen profiles in order of their total scores.

   Keep the profiles with the same total score together, followed by the profiles with the next higher total score, and so on. Within each total score level, order the profiles randomly. The subscores within the profiles must be in the same order in every profile, however. It is very helpful to represent each profile in a bar graph to help participants view the test taker's performance holistically rather than one question at a time. Include the total score of the profile and clearly separate the profiles with same total score from the profiles with the next higher total score. Figure 8 shows an example of a profile.

Figure 8. Example of a Profile Page for the Performance Profile Method

Profile XYZ, Total Score = 20

Task	Score 0	1	2	3	4
1. Given a selection of common street signs, student can indicate STOP, EXIT, and WALK				■	
2. Given a piece of lined paper with 6 names on it, student can indicate his or her name, the teacher's name and a classmate's name.			■		
3. Given 5 cards picturing warning signs/signals, student communicates what each sign says to do.			■		
4. Given paper with the words 'Yes', 'No', and 'Hi', can communicate what each word says.					■
5. Given writing implement and lined paper used in class, student writes first name on the line.			■		
6. Given writing implement, lined paper used in class, and word card, copies word onto lined paper		■			
7. Presented with 2 preferred objects, can tell in a sentence which object he or she likes better.		■			
8. Student can communicate in a sentence what he or she does after school.				■	

Rubric

4 - Completes task with 100% accuracy.

3 - Partially completes task. (As defined with each task)

2 - Minimally completes task. (As defined with each task)

1 - Attempts task.

0 - No response.

3. Prepare a packet that includes the questions or tasks in the test, along with the scoring rubrics. Also include sample responses for each task at each score level to help the participants understand the meaning of each score on each task.

   Select the sample responses to be typical of responses receiving the scores that they received. For example, use a typical 1-point response, a typical 2-point response, and so forth. If the participants are not already familiar with the content and scoring of the test, the selection of these sample responses is critical. They provide the participants with a basis for connecting the numerical scores on the individual questions to test takers' actual performances. If the questions are not weighted equally in computing the total score for a profile, include an explanation of the weighting plan. You will need a copy of this packet for each participant.

4. Give each participant (a) an Ordered Profile Booklet, (b) a packet of questions, rubrics, and sample responses, (c) a copy of the performance level descriptors, and (d) a form to record his or her judgments. Have the participants review the materials. Tell the participants that in the Ordered Profile Booklet the profiles have been arranged in order of total score and that all of the selected profiles with the same total score have been placed together.

5. Have the participants read through the Ordered Profile Booklet, examine each profile, and find the first profile that represents the performance of a borderline test taker for the performance level to be judged first. If the performance levels are Basic, Proficient, and Advanced, many facilitators begin with the Proficient level because the most important distinction is the one between Basic and Proficient. The first round is done individually by the participants.

6. Tell participants to write down the total score level of the first profile in the Ordered Profile Booklet that represents performance that is just barely good enough to be in a performance level (for example, the first profile that is good enough to be called Proficient).

7. Tell participants to then examine all of the profiles in the Ordered Profile Booklet with the same total score as the profile they selected, and decide whether or not all of the profiles at that score level are acceptable as examples of

performance within the performance level. For example, are all the profiles at that total score good enough to be Proficient?

It is possible that a participant will judge some profiles at a score level good enough to be in a performance level, and will judge other profiles with the same total score to be below the performance level. For example, three of the five score profiles with a total of 18 points may be judged to be good enough to be Proficient, but two of them may be judged not good enough to be Proficient.

If some participants find both Proficient and Basic profiles at the same score level, tell those participants that they need to decide whether it is better to label all of the test takers with that total score as Proficient, or to label all of the test takers with that total score as Basic.

If the participants decide to classify all of the profiles with a score of, for example, 18 as Proficient, then they write down the score of 18 on their recording form as their cutscore for the Proficient performance level.

If the participants decide it is preferable to classify all of the profiles with a score of 18 as Basic, then they evaluate profiles with a total score of 19, a total score of 20, and so forth until they find the first score level where they believe it is preferable to classify all of the profiles with the same total score as Proficient. If they decide to classify all profiles with a score of 19 and all profiles with a total score of 20 as Basic, but classify all profiles with a score of 21 as Proficient, they write 21 points on their recording form as the cutscore for the Proficient performance level.

It is a good idea to have participants check the profiles in the score level just above the score level in which all profiles were classified as Proficient to ensure that the selected score level really is the one at which the profiles have consistently changed to Proficient. Participants then go back to Step 6 and repeat the process for the next performance level. If most participants find that there is no clear positive relationship between profile score and performance level (i.e., if higher scores are not associated with higher performance levels), we would suggest you try a different method of setting cutscores.

8. We recommend two or three rounds of profile review with discussion between rounds.

At the end of round 1, give the participants information on how their selected score profiles compared to the selected profiles of the other participants. Tell the participants to discuss the discrepancies. Focus the discussions on which type of misclassification is more acceptable. If you choose to have three rounds of judgments, again compare the participants' cutscores and have the participants discuss which type of misclassification is preferable after the second round. Provide impact data at this stage or after round 1 if you have only two rounds. Tell participants to take their colleagues' opinions and the impact data into account as they make their final judgments, but to make up their own minds about the most appropriate scores to use as the cutscores.

9. Calculate the cutscore. Following the final round, obtain the score level of the profiles that a participant selected to represent acceptable performance for the first performance level to be judged. Do the same for each participant. Calculate the median score value across all participants as the recommended cutscore for the performance level. Then repeat the process for the second performance level to be judged, and so forth.

6.9 Procedures for the Dominant Profile Method

The procedures we describe are designed to help a group of participants reach consensus on a set of decision rules. There are other methods of bringing groups to consensus and you should feel free to modify the procedures to make them more effective in your particular circumstances. Seating participants in groups of 5–8 at separate tables may encourage discussion.

Before participants make any judgments about test questions, be sure the participants understand the performance level descriptors, and the meaning of borderline performance for each performance level. The participants should also be familiar with the test questions.

1. Tell the participants which questions contribute to each subscore. Ask the participants to discuss the knowledge and skills measured by the different subscores and to decide, for each subscore, whether it is necessary to specify a minimum level of competency. We recommend that you provide the

participants with sample test taker responses that illustrate performance on each question at each score level.

2. Demonstrate some of the possibilities for combining total test and subscore cutscores. Your examples should not be overly complicated. Straightforward rules work better than complicated rules. Encourage the participants to use the simplest set of rules they are willing to accept. The more complicated the rules are, the more difficult it is to explain the rules and to apply them.

3. Ask participants to write a decision rule for the cutscore for each performance level, working individually, without discussing their work with the other participants. The rules may involve a minimum score on one or more subscores, and/or a minimum total score on the test.

4. Have participants share their decision rules with others at their table. Encourage the participants to discuss their differences and to reach agreement on one set of decision rules for each table. If agreement cannot be reached at a table, you may have to proceed with more than one set of decision rules per table.

5. Present the decision rules resulting from the deliberations at each table to the total group. Identify the major differences among the proposed decision rules and work with the total group to resolve the differences and to produce one set of decision rules for all participants.

6. Provide impact data for the interim decision rules resulting from Step 5.[34] Allow the participants at each table to deliberate. Be prepared to provide impact data for revised decision rules as the participants continue their discussions and arrive at new interim decision rules. Present the decision rules resulting from the deliberations at each table to the total group. Identify the major differences among the proposed decision rules and work with the total group to resolve the differences and to produce one set of decision rules for all participants.

---

[34] This is going to require your statistician to be on hand and to have the data and software available to provide impact data for any given set of decision rules.

7. We suggest that, once the participants determine the total group's set of decision rules, you give the participants an opportunity to review some test takers' responses that would be within each performance level based on the decision rules. The examples of actual test takers' responses will help participants determine whether or not their decision rules are appropriate. It will be important, therefore, to have test takers' work available to illustrate the test performance that meets various decision rules.

8. After participants review the test takers' responses that meet the decision rules, ask if the participants desire any changes to the decision rules. Try to reach consensus on a set of decision rules.

9. Determine the decision rules for the cutscore. This method results in a group-determined set of decision rules for assigning test takers to performance levels on the basis of the test takers' scores and subscores. The decision rules are determined directly through consensus. If there are differences among the participants it is usually not possible to calculate an average. It is necessary for participants to arrive at a consensus through compromise. If they are unable to reach a compromise, you may have to use a different method to set the cutscore.

6.10 Procedures for the Borderline Group Method

Your statistician can advise you as to how many borderline test takers you will need in your sample to get a stable estimate of the median test score for borderline test takers in general. The number depends on how much the borderline test takers' scores vary. The more variation in the sample, the larger the sample you will need (and the less confident you can be that they are all borderline test takers.)

If most of the test scores of the borderline test takers for a proficiency level are clustered close together, then the method is working well. But if the scores of the borderline group are spread widely over the range of possible scores, then the method is not working well.

You can apply the Borderline Group method by the following sequence of steps:

1. Define borderline levels of the knowledge and skills tested in each performance level.

2. Have the participants identify borderline test takers for each performance level under consideration.

3. Obtain the test scores of the borderline test takers at each performance level.

   If most of the test scores of the borderline test takers for a proficiency level are clustered close together, then the method is working well. But if the scores of the borderline group are spread widely over the range of possible scores, then the method is not working well. Several factors can cause the Borderline Group method to work poorly.

   - The borderline group may include many test takers who do not belong in it. The participants may have identified several test takers as borderline because their skills were difficult to judge or because the participants did not know them well.

   - The participants may be basing their judgments on something other than what the test measures.

   - The participants may differ considerably in their individual standards for judging the test takers.

   You may be able to avoid the first problem by reminding the participants not to include in the borderline group any test takers whose skills they are not familiar with. You can remind participants that it is better to name no test takers than to name any that are not borderline. You can minimize the second and third problems by giving the participants appropriate instructions and by getting them to agree with each other, before making their judgments, on a definition of borderline knowledge and skills.

   A wide range of test scores in a group that is supposed to consist of only borderline test takers implies that the people in the group cannot all be borderline test takers. The usual measure of the amount of variation in the scores of a group of test takers is the standard deviation. Your statistician can calculate the standard deviation of the scores of all the test takers and of each participant's borderline test takers. To avoid basing the cutscore on test takers who are not really members of the borderline group, you may wish to use a decision rule such as requiring the standard deviation of the borderline group to be less than some fraction (e.g., ½) of the standard deviation of the total group. Consult with your statistician to find an appropriate maximum allowable value of the standard deviation of scores of the borderline group. If the standard deviation of the borderline group is almost as large as the standard deviation of scores of all test takers, the method is clearly not working and you should select a different method of setting cutscores.

4. Calculate the Cutscore.

We recommend that you set the cutscore for each performance level at the median test score of the borderline group. If each participant nominated several borderline test takers, you should calculate the median for each participant, and then take the median of the medians as the cutscore. This procedure allows you to see how closely the participants agreed with each other and to identify any participants whose cutscores are substantially different from those of the other participants.

If, however, each participant nominated only 2 or 3 test takers, the individual participants' cutscores will not be very informative. In that case we think it is better to pool all of the scores and take the median of the pooled group as the cutscore. Use the median because a test taker with a very high or very low score compared to the others in the group is likely to be someone who did not really belong in the borderline group.

6.11 Procedures for the Contrasting Groups Method

You can apply the Contrasting Groups method by the following sequence of steps:

1. Define the performance levels to be differentiated by cutscores (Basic and Proficient, for example).

2. Select the sample of test takers whose skills will be judged. You can omit this step if you can get judgments of all the test takers. In most cases, however, it will not be practical to get judgments of all test takers or all test takers' products. You will have to choose a cutscore on the basis of a sample. How should you choose the sample of test takers to be judged?

130

If you have to choose the sample before the test takers' scores are available, you should try for a representative sample of all the people or products. (One way is to choose them at random, for example, by lottery.) But if you can choose them *after* they have taken the test, there is a better way. You can choose the people or products so that their scores are spread evenly throughout the portion of the score range where the cutscore might possibly be located. For example, on a 100-question test, you might choose 10 test takers from each five-point score interval (31–35, 36–40, etc.). The important principle to remember is that the sample of test takers or products you select *at each test score level* must be representative of all the test takers or products *at that test score level.*

One question that test users often ask about the Contrasting Groups method is, "How many test takers do I need?" The only honest answer to this question is, "It depends." Deciding how many test takers to include in a Contrasting Groups study generally involves a tradeoff between costs and benefits. The costs are those of getting the judgments. Judging more test takers will require either more participants or more time from each participant. It may also require time from more of the test takers, if the judgments are based on direct observation of their performances. The benefits of a larger sample are better representation of the test taker population and greater precision in determining the cutscore. The degree of precision you can get with a given number of test takers depends on the extent to which:

> The important principle to remember is that the sample of test takers or products you select at each test score level must be representative of all the test takers or products at that test score level.

- the participants all have the same standards
- the participants apply their standards consistently in judging the test takers
- the test scores and the judgments reflect the same abilities of the test takers
- the test takers' observed performance matches their typical performance

The degree of precision you need will depend on the consequences of the cutscore and the number of people who will be affected by it. It will also depend on how fine a distinction you are trying to make. A choice between cutscores of 3 and 4 on a five-point test is much easier to make, but also much more important, than a choice between cutscores of 73 and 74 on a 100-point test.

The costs of getting judgments of individual test takers, the precision that a given number of test takers will provide, and the need for precision in setting the cutscore will all vary from one testing situation to another. Therefore, we cannot prescribe a minimum number of test takers that will apply to all testing situations. We suggest that you (1) include as many test takers as you can afford to, and (2) consult your statistician for advice that will apply to your testing situation. We cannot offer a strict rule, but we believe it is wise to get judgments in the neighborhood of at least 100 or so test takers for each cutscore you have to set.

3. Ask the participants to judge the performance level of the test takers you have selected. The judgment can be based on evaluation of a work product, evaluation of some performance, or based on knowledge of what the test taker knows and can do. Do *not* let the participants know the test takers' scores.

   Should the participants all judge the same test takers, or should each participant judge a different sample of test takers? If teachers are judging their students, or if supervisors are judging their employees, based on long-term observations of the students' or employees' behavior, you will be able to obtain only one judgment per test taker. In that case, each participant will judge a different sample of test takers.

   If, however, participants are judging samples of the work produced by test takers, such as answers to essay questions, recorded musical performances, architectural drawings, and the like, then you will have a choice about whether participants should all judge the same sample of work products, or if each participant should judge a different sample of work products.

   The main reason for having each participant judge a different sample of products is to increase the total number of test takers represented in the process. The larger the number of test takers, the less the danger that the cutscore will depart substantially from what it would be if participants could judge every possible test taker. It is generally a good idea to include as many test takers as possible in the judging process. Of course, including an additional ten test takers in the data will be a much greater improvement if you have only 40 than it will be if you already have 200.

The main advantage to having all the participants judge the same sample of products is the opportunity for the participants to discuss their disagreements, possibly resolve some of those disagreements, and revise their judgments. The result is likely to be greater consensus among the participants. If there is time to have each participant judge the products of 100 or more test takers, it may be worthwhile to have all the participants judge the same test takers.

In some cases, a compromise is possible. It may be possible to design the study so that each participant judges a different sample of test takers' products, but with some overlap among the samples, i.e., with some of the test takers' products judged by several judges. This overlap in the samples provides an opportunity for comparisons and discussion, which may lead to greater consistency among the individual participants. The overlap in the samples allows you to evaluate the consistency of the judgments that participants make about the overlapping products. For example, you could calculate the percent of participants who classified the products the same way. If you use several rounds of judgments, it is useful to evaluate the consistency of the participants' judgments after each round. If the cutscore method is working well, the consistency of judgments should increase from round to round.

4. Obtain the test scores of the test takers you have selected.

5. Decide whether to analyze the data separately for each participant or to combine the data from all of the participants.

If all the participants judge the same test takers, computing a separate cutscore for each participant will clearly reveal the differences among the participants' individual standards. Even if the participants each make judgments about a different sample of test takers, this kind of computation will provide useful information, if each participant judges enough test takers to imply an approximate cutscore. (Fifty would almost surely be enough for the purpose of calculating a participant's approximate cutscore; thirty or possibly even fewer might be sufficient if the judgments are strongly consistent with the test scores.)

Having a separate cutscore for each participant enables you to compute the median or the trimmed mean of the individual cutscores, reducing the influence of participants with unusually high or low standards. However, if the judgment process is slow and the time available is limited, each participant may have time to judge only a small number of test takers. In this case, the judgments of an individual participant may not clearly imply even an approximate cutscore. In this case, you will need to combine the data from all the participants into a single analysis and compute a single cutscore for the group.

Steps 6–8 form a sequence that has to be done separately for each cutscore. We will use the cutscore between Basic and Proficient as an example.

6. Compute the percentage of the test takers at each score level who are judged to be in the Proficient level or higher. If you do not have several test takers at each score level, combine score levels into larger intervals before you do this calculation.

7. Use a "smoothing" method (explained below) to adjust the percentages you have computed.

   When you compute the percentage of the test takers at each test score level who are Proficient or higher, you may find that the percentage does not increase steadily from one test score to the next. Instead, it may follow a zigzag pattern. This kind of result is especially likely if the number of test takers at each score level is small. It seems reasonable to assume that if you could get judgments of all possible test takers, the percent who are at least Proficient would increase steadily from one test score level to the next (possibly leveling off at the extreme score levels).

   What you need, then, is a way to adjust the percentages to bring them closer to what you would have found if you had obtained test scores and judgments of all possible test takers. The general term for adjustments of this kind is "smoothing." There are several techniques for smoothing observed percentages. We will describe some simple

134

smoothing techniques. You should consult your statistician to determine if more complex smoothing techniques would be more appropriate for your data. Figure 9 below shows an example of observed data and the results of smoothing the data.

Figure 9. Observed and Smoothed Data

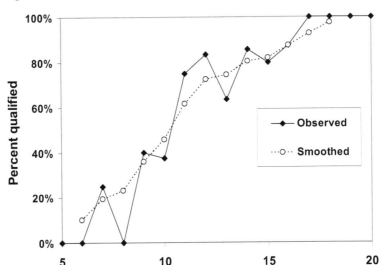

All smoothing methods are based on the idea that the judgments of test takers at each test score level tell you something about the knowledge and skills of test takers at nearby test score levels. One smoothing method that is easy to apply is to draw a graph showing the percentages as points. Then try to draw a smooth curve that comes as close to the points as possible and read the smoothed percentages from the graph. This technique is called "graphic smoothing." It is subjective. Different people applying the method could come up with different results. Nevertheless, it tends to produce results that are similar to the results of methods of smoothing based on numerical calculations.

> *All smoothing methods are based on the idea that the judgments of test takers at each test score level tell you something about the knowledge and skills of test takers at nearby test score levels.*

Most computational smoothing methods calculate a smoothed percentage at each test score level, except the lowest and the highest. One common technique is to average the data at each score level with the data from the next lower and next higher score levels, or possibly the next two lower and the next two higher score levels. This kind of smoothing is called "moving-average smoothing." See Figures 10 and 11 for an example of moving-average smoothing.

Figure 10. Data for Example of Smoothing

Score Range	Number Qualified	Number Unqualified	Total	Percent Qualified
96-100	5	0	5	5/5 = 100%
91-95	3	1	4	3/4 = 75%
86-90	6	2	8	6/8 = 75%
81-85	18	1	19	18/19 = 95%
76-80	17	3	20	17/20 = 85%
71-75	15	10	25	15/25 = 60%
66-70	20	9	29	20/29 = 69%
61-65	7	8	15	7/15 = 47%
56-60	6	17	23	6/23 = 26%
51-55	2	9	11	2/11 = 18%
46-50	6	8	14	6/14 = 43%
41-45	2	4	6	2/6 = 33%
36-40	2	12	14	2/14 = 14%
31-35	0	7	7	0
0-30	0	3	3	0

Figure 11. Example of Smoothing By Moving Average

Score Range	Number Qualified	Total	Smoothed Percent Qualified
96-100	5	5	*
91-95	3	4	(5+3+6) / (5+4+8) = 82%
86-90	6	8	(3+6+18) / (4+8+19) = 87%
81-85	18	19	(6+18+17) / (8+19+20) = 87%
76-80	17	20	(18+17+15) / (19+20+25) = 78%
71-75	15	25	(17+15+20) / (20+25+29) = 70%
66-70	20	29	(15+20+7) / (25+29+15) = 61%
61-65	7	15	…and so forth

*This method cannot be used at the highest and lowest score levels.

An improvement on this method is to weight the test takers unequally in computing the smoothed percentage, giving the test takers at the score level for which you are estimating the smoothed percentage a heavier weight than the test takers at the nearby levels. The closer the test takers' scores are to the test score level for which you are computing the smoothed percentage, the more heavily they count in the calculation. For example, you might use a weighted average of the test takers from two levels below to two levels above the score level for which you are calculating the smoothed percentage, with weights of 1, 2, 4, 2, and 1. This kind of smoothing is called "weighted moving-average smoothing."

There are many smoothing methods, and most statistical software packages offer a choice of methods. Some of these smoothing methods impose the restriction that a graph of the smoothed percentages must have a particular shape. For choosing a cutscore, we prefer smoothing methods that do not impose such a restriction, although it is reasonable to require that the smoothed percentages do not decrease as the test scores increase.

Different smoothing methods can result in different cutscores. Although these differences will tend to be small, you may want to keep the process as objective as possible by specifying which smoothing method you will use before you collect the data. You may find that the resulting curve is not as smooth as you would like, but you will be protected against the charge that you deliberately chose a smoothing method that would produce a particular cutscore.

8. Choose the cutscore on the basis of the "smoothed" percentage.

The final step in applying the Contrasting Groups method is to choose the cutscores. This method enables you to take account of the possibility that the two types of misclassifications may not have equally serious consequences. For example, is it more harmful to classify a Proficient student as Basic than it is to classify a Basic student as Proficient?

The policymakers may wish to make such decisions themselves, or they may want you to complete the task and produce provisional cutscores that they can later adjust. It is a good idea to determine the policymakers' preference for involvement before you reach this stage of the process.

One logical choice for the cutscore that separates Basic from Proficient is the test score for which the "smoothed" percent Proficient (or higher) is exactly 50 percent. At any lower test-score level, a test taker is more likely to be judged Basic (or lower) than Proficient (or higher), while the reverse is true at any higher test-score level.

The rationale for setting the cutscore at the test score that corresponds to a 50 percent chance of being judged Proficient is based on the assumption that the two types of possible wrong decisions about a test taker are equally serious. But if they are not equally serious, what should you do? Statistical decision theory (which, at its simplest levels, is really common sense expressed in mathematical language) provides an answer to this question.

If it is twice as bad to classify a Basic test taker as Proficient as it is to classify a Proficient test taker as Basic, then the best choice for the cutscore would be the test score at which there are exactly two Proficient test takers for every Basic test taker. This would be the test score that corresponds to 67 percent Proficient. By similar reasoning, if it were three times as bad to classify a Basic test taker as Proficient as it is to classify a Proficient test taker as Basic, the cutscore would be the test score at which Proficient test takers outnumber Basic test takers by three to one. That would be the test score that corresponds to 75 percent Proficient. On the other hand, classifying a Proficient test taker as Basic might be the more serious of the two types of errors (for example, if the test takers classified as Basic will receive a very expensive remedial training program). In this case, you might want to lower the cutscore to the test-score level where Basic test takers outnumber Proficient test takers by two to one or three to one.

> **The rationale for setting the cutscore at the test score that corresponds to a 50 percent chance of being judged Proficient is based on the assumption that the two types of possible wrong decisions about a test taker are equally serious.**

138

In practice, you may find it simpler to ask the persons who are responsible for choosing the cutscore, "Suppose you had a group of 100 test takers and you knew that 50 were Basic and 50 were Proficient. If you had to classify all 100 as Basic, or classify all 100 as Proficient, which would you do?" If they are undecided, you will know that the cutscore you seek is the point that corresponds to 50 percent Proficient. If the answer is "classify them as Basic," then ask the same question about a group of 70 Proficient test takers and 30 Basic test takers. If the answer is now "classify them as Proficient," ask the same question about a group of 60 Proficient test takers and 40 Basic test takers. Keep adjusting the percent Proficient in this way until you have found the percentage at which the decision makers cannot decide whether the test takers should be classified as Basic or Proficient. The test score that gives you that percentage will be the cutscore.

6.12 Procedures for the Up and Down Modification of the Contrasting Groups Method

Use the following procedures to apply the Up and Down modification in a Contrasting Groups study. We will use the terms Proficient and Basic to refer to the contrasting groups in setting the Proficient cutscore. Please read section 6.11, *Procedures for the Contrasting Groups Method*, before continuing.

1. Select a test taker with a test score near the middle of the score distribution. Have the participant judge this test taker's work product such as an answer to an essay question, or a painting, without seeing the test score.

2. If the participant judges the first test taker's work product to represent work at the Proficient level, select next a test taker with a somewhat lower test score. If the participant judges the test taker's product to be at the Basic level select next a test taker with a somewhat higher test score, but not as high as that of the first test taker. Have the participant judge this test taker's work product.

   Repeat step 2 until you have as many judgments from this participant as you need (or as many as you can afford). It is best not to stop until you have observed several "reversals." A reversal is a judgment of Proficient preceded by a judgment of Basic, or vice versa.

If the test score scale has many possible scores with only a few test takers at each score level, it may be necessary to combine score levels by creating two-point intervals, or three-point intervals, or five-point intervals. For example, if the test score scale extends from 1 to 100, it might be necessary to combine the scores into five-point intervals of 1 to 5, 6 to 10, 11 to 15, etc. These intervals would be used to select test takers for judging, but in the cutscore calculations, you would use the actual test scores.

One important choice in applying the Up and Down method is the step size—the difference between the score of the last test taker judged and the next test taker to be judged. (If the score scale is divided into intervals as suggested above, the step size could be one interval, or two intervals, or possibly more.) If the step size is too small, it may take many judgments to move to the test score range where the cutscore should be. But if the step size is too large, it will be difficult to determine a cutscore with much precision. One practical approach is to begin with a large step size and, after five or so reversals, switch to a smaller step size.

3. Calculate the cutscore. The cutscore is calculated as it is in the Contrasting Groups method described in section 6.11.

6.13 Procedures for the Body of Work Method

Before participants make any judgments about the responses to test questions, be sure the participants understand the performance level descriptors for each performance level. The participants should also be familiar with the test questions and the scoring rubrics. Steps 1 and 2 must be completed before the beginning of the cutscore meeting.

1. Obtain Response Booklets for the participants to evaluate.

   Usually, there will be many more Response Booklets available after a test administration than you need for the cutscore study. If the responses have been double scored, select only those responses on which the scorers agreed. Select approximately 10 Booklets across the range of scores obtained by test takers to use for the practice round. Then, select an additional 30 Booklets spread across the range of obtained scores for the range-finding round. Select only one very low score and one very high score for this group of Booklets. For the pin-pointing round, you will need more

140

Response Booklets at score levels that depend on the participants' judgments during the range-finding round. It is difficult to determine exactly which score values you need ahead of time. We recommend selecting at least two Booklets for every possible score point, excluding the very lowest and very highest points. You will not need many Response Booklets with extremely high or extremely low scores, because no cutscores are likely to be set at those parts of the score scale. If you have a smaller range of score values, consider selecting three Booklets per score value.

You will need to make arrangements to obtain and copy Response Booklets rapidly during the study for the pin-pointing round. If the Response Booklets are actually CDs, DVDs, slides, or anything other than written pages, you will need special copying equipment and staff who know how to use the equipment, or you will need multiple copies of the Response Booklets of every possible score level on hand. You will also need copies of the tests, the scoring rubrics, and the performance level descriptors—enough copies of each to give one copy to each participant.

2. Prepare the Response Booklets to be used for the practice and range-finding rounds.

The assignment of Response Booklets to performance levels should be based on the match between the knowledge and skills demonstrated in the Response Booklet and the knowledge and skills required to be in a performance level.

Put an easily seen, unique identifier on each Response Booklet, so you will be able to refer to the Booklet by "name" in discussions with the participants. (A two-digit ID number or letter code is convenient. Do *not* number the Response Booklets in the order of their scores. The identifiers should give no information about the scores of the Response Booklets.) Make enough copies of each selected Response Booklet to give one copy to each participant.

3. To begin the practice round, give each participant a copy of a set of 5 to 8 Response Booklets, selected to include examples from all of the performance levels. All of the participants should get the same Response Booklets. Do *not*

tell the participants the scores of the Response Booklets. Ask the participants to study the materials in each Response Booklet carefully and, working independently, to assign each Response Booklet to a performance level. The assignment of Response Booklets to performance levels should be based on the match between the knowledge and skills demonstrated in the Response Booklet and the knowledge and skills required to be in a performance level.

4. Have the participants state their results. Display the cumulative results for the participants to see. Encourage the participants to discuss their differences and to specify why they placed particular Response Booklets in particular performance levels. Allow the participants to change their assignments of Response Booklets to performance levels if they desire to do so after hearing the comments of their colleagues. Update the display to reflect any changes the participants make. Figure 12 shows an example of the results of a practice round.

Figure 12. Hypothetical Results of Body of Work Practice Exercise

Booklet ID	Score	Number of participants classifying booklet as ...		
		Basic	Proficient	Advanced
36	5	19		
54	14	16	3	
11	22	2	17	
69	27	1	18	
21	32		2	17
45	38		2	17

5. Tell the participants the scores of the Response Booklets. Post the results on the display and encourage discussion of any large discrepancies between the score of a Response Booklet and the performance level to which it is assigned.

For example, if some participants placed a high scoring Response Booklet in a low performance category, ask the participants to say what characteristics of the Response Booklet influenced their judgment and why they put it in the category they selected. If some participants placed a low scoring Response Booklet in a high performance category, ask the participants to say what characteristics of the Response Booklet influenced their judgment. Allow participants to change their assignments. Show the participants how a cutscore would be calculated (see Step 16) based on the participants' assignments of Response Booklets to categories. This step ends the practice round.

6. For the range-finding round, select about 30 new Response Booklets having scores that span the full range of scores actually obtained by test takers. Give each participant a copy of each Response Booklet. Do not let the participants know the scores of the Response Booklets.

7. Ask the participants to assign each Response Booklet to a performance level, working independently. Tell the participants to base the assignment of Response Booklets to performance levels on the match between the knowledge and skills demonstrated in the Response Booklet and the knowledge and skills required to be in a performance level.

8. Display the results for the participants to see. Encourage the participants to discuss their differences and to specify why they placed particular Response Booklets in particular performance levels. Allow the participants to change their assignments of Response Booklets to performance levels if they desire to do so after hearing the comments of their colleagues. Update the display to reflect any changes made by the participants.

9. Display the scores of the Response Booklets placed in each performance level. If any participants placed a Response Booklet in a performance level where all (or nearly all) of the other Booklets have much lower scores or much higher scores, ask the participants who placed it there to say why they think it belongs there. Allow the participants to change their assignments of those Booklets to performance levels if they desire to do so.

10. Use the results of the range-finding round to determine roughly where the cutscores are likely to be. We will call this region the *probable cutscore range*. The cutscore separating two performance levels is likely to be somewhere in the region between the highest score of any Response Booklet placed in the lower performance level, and the lowest score of any Response Booklet placed in the higher performance level. For example, if the *highest* score of any

Response Booklet classified as Basic is 55, and the *lowest* score of any Response Booklet classified as Proficient is 46, then the cutscore between Basic and Proficient is likely to be somewhere between 46 and 55. Be sure the participants are comfortable with the probable cutscore range they will be reviewing in the next round before continuing. If a participant wants to extend the range, do so.

11. For the pin-pointing round, give the participants two new Response Booklets at each score point in each of the probable cutscore ranges identified in the range-finding round and also at the score points that are one point above and below each range. For example, if the Basic-Proficient probable cutscore range is 46 to 55, you would give the participants two Response Booklets at scores of 45, two Response Booklets at scores of 46, and so forth, ending with two Response Booklets at scores of 56 (a total of 24 new Response Booklets). Order the test books randomly before you give them to the participants. Do *not* let the participants know the scores at this time. Ask the participants to place each new Response Booklet into either the Basic or the Proficient category.

12. Continue with the next probable cutscore range. For example, if the Proficient-Advanced probable cutscore range is 68 to 75, you would give the participants two new Response Booklets at each of the score points 67 to 76 (another 20 new Response Booklets). Do not reveal the scores at this time. Ask the participants to place each Response Booklet into either the Proficient category or the Advanced category.[35] Encourage the participants to discuss the results of their placements.

13. Display the results of the judgments for the participants. Encourage the participants to discuss their differences and

---

[35] You can reduce the number of Response Booklets you have to reproduce by dividing the participants into two groups, giving one group the Basic-Proficient Response Booklets to classify and giving the other group the Proficient-Advanced Response Booklets. When both groups have finished, have the groups trade booklets. This procedure can be inefficient in its use of the participants' time if the groups work at markedly different speeds, but it does save a lot of copying.

144

to specify why they placed particular Response Booklets in particular performance levels. Allow the participants to change their assignments of Response Booklets to performance levels if they desire to do so after hearing the comments of their colleagues

14. Display the results, including the scores of the Response Booklets, for all the participants to see. Encourage further discussion among the participants. Give them the opportunity to change their assignments of Booklets to Performance levels if they want to.

15. If impact data are available, provide impact data to the participants at this stage and have another round of pin-pointing judgments.

16. Calculate the cutscore.

Pool the judgments of all the participants in the final round into a data set for your statistician. For example, a convenient way to organize the data set is to have a separate record for each judgment, identifying the participant who made the judgment, the Response Booklet judged, and the performance level it was judged to belong in.

An obvious choice for the cutscore between two performance levels is the score at which a Booklet is just as likely to be placed into the higher performance level as in the lower performance level.

To find the cutscore between adjacent performance levels, first estimate for every score in the probable cutscore range the probability that a Response Booklet with that score would be classified into the higher performance level. One way to estimate those probabilities, and the way the estimation is typically done for the Body of Work method, is to use a statistical procedure called *logistic regression*. Logistic regression gives you, for every score, the probability that the Booklet is in the higher performance level. Your statistician can do the calculation for you.

You could also find the cutscore as described above for the Contrasting Groups method (section 6.11), by (1) grouping the Response Booklets into score intervals; (2) computing, for each score interval, the percentage of Response Booklets classified into the higher performance level;

(3) smoothing the percentages; and (4) choosing the cutscore that corresponds to a specified percentage.

An obvious choice for the cutscore between two performance levels is the score at which a Booklet is just as likely to be placed into the higher performance level as in the lower performance level. This is the point at which the estimated probability that a booklet will be classified into the higher performance level is .50. Alternatively, the participants can provide their judgments about the relative harm of the two types of misclassifications, so the cutscore that causes the least harm can be identified, as described for the Contrasting Groups method.

6.14 Procedures for the Analytic Judgment Method

Before participants make any judgments about the responses to test questions, be sure the participants understand the performance level descriptors, and the meaning of borderline performance for each performance level. The participants should also be familiar with the test questions.

Steps 1–3 should be accomplished before the cutscore meeting begins.

1. Divide the test into parts so that the participants can review and judge the responses to each part separately. These parts could be naturally occurring sections of the test. If there are constructed response questions with extended responses, each question could be a separate part of the test. If you prefer, you could divide the test into meaningful subparts such as questions based on a common stimulus, questions measuring the same content areas, questions with the same formats, and so forth.

2. Select responses for judgment that represent the whole range of performance on each part of the test. Label each response with an easily seen unique identifier such as a number or letter code so you will be able to refer to the response by "name" in discussions with the participants. The identifier should indicate the question(s) on which the response is based, but the identifier should not be associated with the score given to the response. Try to obtain about 50 responses to each part of the test. You will need the scores of each response to calculate the cutscore, but the participants should not see the scores.

146

3. You have to decide how to assign the responses to participants. Having every participant judge every response will allow the whole group to participate in discussions of the same responses and give you the most stable averages. Alternatively, you could save time by dividing the participants into subgroups and having each subgroup judge a different set of test questions. For example, you could give half of the responses to one half of the participants and the other half of the responses to the other half of the participants. This will allow discussion of the same responses only within each subset of participants. More responses will be judged per unit of time, but each response will be judged by fewer participants. As a compromise, you could give each group some responses in common with the other group and some responses specific to each group. Make a copy of each selected response for each of the participants who will be judging that response.

4. Give the first set of responses to the participants. Ask the participants to work independently to (1) assign each response to a performance level, and (2) to further categorize the response as low, medium, or high within the assigned performance level.[36] Some participants may prefer

Figure 13. Categorization of Responses by Performance Level

Level	Response IDs
Basic	
Low	
Medium	
High	
Proficient	
Low	
Medium	
High	
Advanced	
Low	
Medium	
High	

[36] Some modifications of this procedure ask participants to ignore the distinction between the low and medium categories in the lowest performance level and the distinction between the medium and high categories in the highest performance level.

to do the task in one step rather than select a performance level first and then further categorize the response. That is acceptable. Participants may be given a form to use such as the one shown in Figure 13 (on the previous page), for example. They place the identifier of each response into the appropriate cell.

5. Display the decisions made by all of the participants. If participants did not agree on the placement of the responses, ask the participants who had relatively high or low placements to explain the reasons for their decisions. Encourage discussion of the appropriate placement. Tell the participants that they are free to change the placement of the response on their individual forms, but they do not have to do so. See Figure 14 for an example of the display of the participants' decisions.

6. Repeat the process for the responses to the next part of the test. Continue, part by part, until the responses for the whole

Figure 14. Display of Participants' Judgments at the Basic/Proficient Cutscore Using the Analytic Judgment Method for a Test with Three Sections.

Response ID	Score	Number of participants classifying response as ...								
		Basic			Proficient			Advanced		
		Low	Med.	High	Low	Med.	High	Low	Med.	High
M25	5		5	3	2					
M18	6		2	6	2					
M06	7			5	5					
M29	8			3	6	1				
M12	9			2	5	3				
M15	10			0	6	3	1			
P25	2		7	3	0					
P13	3		5	4	1					
P02	4		1	5	3	1				
P21	5			7	3					
P11	6			9	1					
P15	7				9	1				
T25	10		8	1	1					
T18	11		6	4						
T06	12		3	5	2					
T29	13			5	4	1				
T12	14			2	6	2				
T15	15				8	1	1			

148

test have been categorized. Alternatively, you can distribute responses to several parts at one time and discuss only those on which there is substantial disagreement.

7. Calculate the cutscores.

Collect the forms from the participants. Pool the participants' judgments for each part of the test. For the first cutscore, obtain the scores of all the responses to the first part of the test that have been placed in the categories adjacent to the borderline between the performance levels that the cutscore will separate, e.g., high Basic and low Proficient.

The most common approach to calculating a cutscore in the Analytic Judgment method is to find the average scores of all the responses to a part of the test that are in the categories adjacent to the borderline between performance levels. For example, find the average score of all the responses to the first part of the test in the high Basic and low Proficient categories. However, If the numbers of responses in each of the borderline categories are unequal (e.g., more responses on the low Proficient side than on the high Basic side), the averaging process shifts the cutscore toward the category that includes more responses.

To avoid that effect, we recommend finding the average score of all the responses to the first part of the test in, for example, the high Basic category. Next, find the average score of all the responses to the first part of the test in the low Proficient category. Then find the point that is midway between those two averages. For example, the cutscore between Basic and Proficient for the first question would be placed midway between the average score of the responses classified as high Basic and the average score of the responses classified as low Proficient.[37]

8. Complete the same calculation for each part of the test. To find the cutscore on the test for the Proficient level, for example, sum the cutscores obtained for each part of the test based on responses in the high Basic and low Proficient categories. To find the cutscore on the test for the Advanced

[37] Some facilitators have employed polynomial model fitting to select the cutscore using a cubic regression to best fit the data. Ask your statistician about the advantages and disadvantages of that approach.

level, for example, sum the cutscores obtained for each part of the test based on responses in the high Proficient and low Advanced categories.

9. Show the participants the resulting cutscore(s), and, if you possibly can, provide impact data. Allow for a group discussion and final changes to the assignment of responses to categories. If the participants make changes, repeat Step 7 with the revised judgments.

6.15 Procedures for Judgments about a Reference Group

You can apply this method by the following sequence of steps:

1. Identify the reference group.

   The reference group should be fairly large (at least 100 or so), so that the judgments of the percentage of the test takers who are in a performance level will not depend heavily on a few of the test takers. You do not need to know the test scores of individual test takers, but you do need to know how many test takers in the group received each test score.

2. Define the knowledge and skills required to be in each performance level.

   Make sure that the participants understand the knowledge and skills required to be in each performance level. This is an important step in the process, in this method as in any other method, because the definitions of the performance levels will determine the meanings of the cutscore.

3. Collect judgments (or data) from the participants about the percentage of the people in the reference group who are in each performance level. (If you have judgments about each individual test taker rather than about the group as a whole, you should use the Contrasting Groups method or the Borderline Group method.)

   The participants can make their judgments individually or as a group. We recommend a compromise procedure. Have each participant make a preliminary judgment of the percent of the reference group that have reached each proficiency level, i.e., the percentage who are at that level *or a higher level*. We call that percentage the "percent qualified" at that proficiency level.

For example, assume that Basic is the lowest level. A participant who believes that 30 percent of the reference group are at the Basic level, 50 percent are at the Proficient level, and 20 percent are at the Advanced level will indicate 100 percent qualified at the Basic level, 70 percent qualified at the Proficient level and 20 percent qualified at the Advanced level.[38]

4. For each proficiency level, display the individual participants' judgments of the percent qualified on a screen, a white board, or a large sheet of paper that the participants can all see.

5. If the individual participants' judgments vary substantially, ask a participant who chose a high number to explain why. Then ask a participant who chose a low number to explain why. Allow discussion, but it is not necessary to have all of the participants reach agreement. Give the participants a chance to change their judgments if they want to, and collect the revised judgments for that proficiency level.

6. Calculate the cutscore.

At each proficiency level, compute the mean, median, or trimmed mean of the individual participants' judgments of the percent in each score level. Your statistician can use the distribution of scores of the reference group on the test to determine the cutscores that would produce (as nearly as possible) the average percentages that you computed.

6.16 Procedures for Judgments About Two Reference Groups

1. Identify the reference groups. For each performance level on which you are setting a cutscore, you will need a qualified group and an unqualified group. The reference groups should be, to the extent possible, similar to the operational test takers. For example, if all of the test takers will have taken a course in psychology, using people who never took a course in psychology as the unqualified group is inappropriate. It is preferable to use people who took the course and performed poorly as the unqualified group.

---

[38] The percent qualified to be in at least the lowest performance level will always be 100 percent.

2. Select a sample of persons from each group and give them the test. The samples should be large enough (at least 50 or so per group), so that the performance of a group will not be determined by a few, possibly atypical, members.

3. To set the cutscore, calculate the median score for each group. Set the cutscore midway between the two medians.

6.17 Procedures for the Beuk Method

To use the Beuk method, ask each participant to answer two questions:

- What should the cutscore be?
- What should the pass rate be?

The first question can be answered by any method that produces a separate cutscore for each participant. In effect, Beuk's method is a way of combining one of those methods with the method based on judgments about a reference group. These two types of judgments will almost never be perfectly consistent with each other. The participants' recommended cutscores will not produce their recommended pass rates—not for the individual participants, and not for the group as a whole.

The logic of the Beuk method is simple but elegant: If the participants agree more about the cutscore than they agree about the pass rate, give more weight to their judgments of the cutscore. If they agree more about the pass rate than they agree about the cutscore, give more weight to their judgments of the pass rate.

Have your statistician do the following:

1. Calculate the mean and standard deviation of the participants' recommended cutscores.

The logic of the Beuk method is simple but elegant: If the participants agree more about the cutscore than they agree about the pass rate, give more weight to their judgments of the cutscore. If they agree more about the pass rate than they agree about the cutscore, give more weight to their judgments of the pass rate.

2. Calculate the mean and standard deviation of the participants' recommended pass rates.

3. Make a graph showing the actual pass rate (Y) that will result from each possible choice of a cutscore (X). This graph will be a descending curve, because the pass rate goes down as the cutscore goes up. (See Figure 15 below for an example.)

4. Plot the point that indicates the mean cutscore and the mean pass rate based on the participants' judgments.

5. Determine the line through that point, with a slope equal to the ratio of the standard deviations of the participants' judgments (as in Figure 15 below).

   Note that the larger the standard deviation of the pass rates (the more disagreement about the pass rates), the steeper the slope of the line. Conversely, the larger the standard deviation of the cutscores (the more disagreement about the cutscores), the shallower the slope of the line.

Figure 15. Graph for Beuk Method

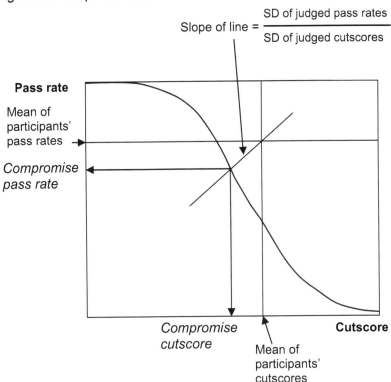

6. Determine the point where that line passes through the decreasing curve that shows the actual pass rate. This point will indicate both the compromise cutscore and the pass rate that will result from using that cutscore.

Although Beuk proposed his method for selecting a single cutscore, it can be used to determine two or more cutscores on the same test, by simply repeating the procedure with a different set of judgments.

6.18 Procedures for the Hofstee Method

In the Hofstee method, each participant must make four judgments:

1. the lowest cutscore that would be acceptable even if everybody passed;

2. the highest cutscore that would be acceptable even if everybody failed;

3. the lowest acceptable pass rate; and

4. the highest acceptable pass rate.

From this point, the method is similar to the Beuk method, except that the line is determined by connecting two points. One point is indicated by the lowest acceptable cutscore and the lowest acceptable pass rate. The other point is indicated by the highest acceptable cutscore and the highest acceptable pass rate. Figure 16 shows the graph for an example of the Hofstee method.

A problem with the Hofstee method is the lack of a convincing rationale for connecting the two points with a straight line rather than some other type of curve. The rectangle in the upper right portion of Figure 16 encloses the points that represent acceptable combinations of cutscore and pass rate. But it is not clear why the combinations represented by points on the diagonal line would be preferable to the combinations represented by other points in the rectangle.

Figure 16. Graph for Hofstee Method

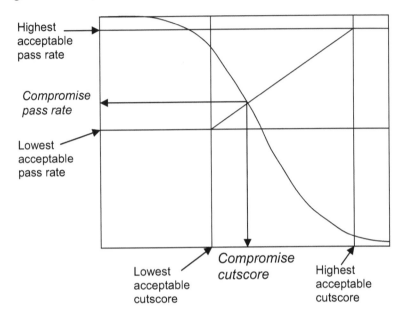

7. WHAT YOU HAVE TO DO AFTER YOU SET THE CUTSCORE

7.1 Review the Cutscore Study

Regardless of the method that you used, review the process by which the cutscore was set before you submit the results of the cutscore study to the policymakers. If something in the process was not right, you will want to find out about it before you go any further. The following questions may help to focus your attention on things that might have gone wrong. For each question in the list below you should be able to provide evidence to support your answer. We strongly recommend that you use the questions to help ensure quality as you are planning and running your study, rather than waiting until the study has been completed and using the questions only at that time.

- Did you have enough participants for a credible study?
- Were the participants all qualified to make the kinds of judgments they were making?
- Were the participants a representative group? Did they reflect the diversity of the population of possible participants?
- Did the participants understand their task?
- Did the participants have enough time to complete their tasks carefully?
- Did all the participants complete all of the required work and complete all of the required forms?
- Did all or almost all of the participants express a reasonable degree of satisfaction with the process and reasonable confidence in the results?
- Were all of the data entered correctly?
- Were all the calculations done correctly?
- Were all of the results reported correctly?
- Did the cutscore study go as planned? Were there any problems that could affect the results? If so, what was done to alleviate the problems? Do you have reason to believe that the remedies worked?

If you find after the study that one or more of the answers is "no," you will have to decide if the problem can be fixed. For example, some errors, such as misreading a participant's

156

Angoff rating for an item, can be corrected after the study because the outcomes of the study would not change in any significant way. If such a problem can be fixed, you should fix it.

Some problems, however, cannot be fixed without running another cutscore study. For example, if you had too many unqualified participants or if the participants did not understand what they were doing, there is no remedy for those severe problems after the cutscore study is completed. You have to start over. Therefore, we reiterate our strong recommendation to raise questions like those listed above before and during the cutscore study, while it is still possible to fix any problems that may be found.

7.2 Document the Cutscore Study

It is very important to produce and retain complete documentation of the cutscore study in a report that can be made available to the public. You should have the documentation available for the policymakers who will use the information from your study to set the operational cutscore. The jurisdiction for which you are setting the cutscore will certainly want a report for its records. Researchers, unions, education reporters, members of advocacy groups, teachers, parents, potential plaintiffs and their lawyers, and some members of the public may be interested in details of the cutscore study, particularly if they do not like the outcomes of using the cutscores. Furthermore, if there is litigation concerning the cutscores, you may be called on to testify about the details of the study long after you have forgotten most of them, and you will need the report to refresh your memory.

It is very important to produce and retain complete documentation of the cutscore study in a report that can be made available to the public.

We recommend that you collect each type of information you will need for your report as soon as it becomes available. Do not wait until the study is over to start gathering data for the report. For example, you will certainly need to document the qualifications of the participants. You should obtain that information before the study and make it ready for insertion in a report as soon as you know who actually attended the study.

Much of the report can be pre-written. For example, you will know what method you will use to set cutscores long before the study takes place. Descriptions of the cutscore method and supporting references can be completed in advance of the study. You can prepare table formats and headers (table shells) in advance to display data such as the results of each round of judgments for each participant. After the study, all you need to do to complete the tables is to plug in the numbers. If you include any confidential materials in the report, such as secure test questions, put them in a separately bound appendix to the report so that the rest of the report can be released to all who are interested.

Your report should provide answers to the following questions, in roughly the following order:

- What organization, agency, or jurisdiction commissioned the study?
- What organization, agency, or jurisdiction conducted the study?
- What tests will cutscores be set for? What is the purpose of the tests? What is the intended population of test takers? When will the tests be given?
- What is the purpose for setting cutscores? What decisions are made on the basis of the cutscores?
- What performance levels and policy definitions were used? What are the performance level descriptors? (Include in appendix.) Who developed them? When and how were they developed?
- When and where was the cutscore study held?
- Who was involved in running the cutscore study? What were each person's responsibilities? What are each person's qualifications?
- Who participated in the cutscore study? How were the participants selected? What were the desired qualifications of the participants? What are their actual qualifications?
- What was the desired distribution of the demographic characteristics of the participants? What is the actual distribution of the demographic characteristics of the participants?
- Who observed the cutscore study?

- Was there an external evaluator? Did the external evaluator produce a report? How can it be accessed?
- What method was used to set the cutscore? Why was the method chosen? (Include supporting references.)
- What materials were sent to participants in advance of the meeting? (Include copies in an appendix.)
- Did the participants take the test? Under what conditions?
- How were the participants trained? What content was included in the training? (Include slides and other materials used in training in an appendix.)
- Was there a practice session before the actual setting of cutscores? Did participants sign statements indicating their readiness to proceed before the actual setting of cutscores. (Include a copy of the form.)
- Did the participants evaluate the training? What were the results of the evaluations? (Include an evaluation form and summary statistics of the evaluations.)
- What are the definitions of borderline performance? (Include in appendix.)
- What materials were given to the participants during the meeting, e.g., Ordered Item Booklets, test booklets, performance level descriptors, etc.? (Include copies of all non-confidential materials in an appendix.)
- How was the method implemented? (Provide a step-by-step description of what was done.)
- What normative data were provided? At what stages of the process?
- What discussions took place among the participants? When were those discussions held?
- How many iterations of judgments were made? How did the distributions of judgments change over time? (Include complete distribution and summary statistics.)
- How were the results combined across participants? What were the group results after each iteration?
- What were the final cutscore recommendations for individual participants (not identified by name) and for the total group? (Include the complete distribution and summary statistics.)

- If the test has been administered, what is the impact of using the final iteration cutscores from the study for the total group of test takers and for important subgroups?
- Did the participants evaluate the cutscore meeting? What were the results? If the participants evaluated the meeting at various stages (e.g., after training, after the first round of judgments, after the last round of judgments) how did the evaluations change from one stage to the next? (Include the evaluation form, summary statistics from the evaluations and any written comments.)

Begin the report with an executive summary of the main points. Take extra care with the summary because many people will read only the summary. The summary and the report as a whole are likely to receive a great deal of public scrutiny, particularly if litigation concerning the cutscore takes place. Obtain reviews of the report for accuracy by someone who attended the entire study, for technical adequacy by an expert in setting cutscores, and for grammatical and stylistic correctness by a professional editor. Keep the raw data that were used to produce the summary statistics that you included in the report. For example, keep the participants' evaluation forms even after the results have been summarized in your report. Do not discard any documents that result from the cutscore study until your lawyer says they are no longer needed.

7.3 Help Policymakers Set the Operational Cutscore

Operational cutscores are set by policymakers who have the legal authority to do so. Your job is to give the policymakers information about the results of the cutscore study to help them make appropriate decisions. To begin with, you should provide information about the quality of the cutscore study. Policymakers are likely to give the results more weight if the study was done using an appropriate method and included a good sample of highly qualified participants. Information about the participants' opinions on the quality of the procedures and their confidence in their recommendations can also influence the policymakers.

> *Operational cutscores are set by policymakers who have the legal authority to do so. Your job is to give the policymakers information about the results of the cutscore study to help them make appropriate decisions.*

160

Show policymakers the percent of students in each performance level using the cutscores recommended by the study. If you have the data, break out the results by various groups such as race or ethnicity, gender, economic status, and so forth. See Figure 17. It is also useful to give the policymakers data showing the percentages of test takers who will be classified into each performance level for several plausible cutscores, centered on the cutscores set at the study. See Figure 18 on the next page.

Figure 17. Shell for Table Showing Percentage of Students in Each Performance Category, Using Cutscores Recommended by Study (Proficient Cut =___; Advanced Cut = ___)

Demographic Group	Number of Students	Mean raw score	Percent Basic	Percent Proficient	Percent Advanced
All Students					
Special needs:					
Special Education					
Limited English Proficient					
No special needs					
Gender:					
Female					
Male					
Race/ethnicity:					
American Indian					
Asian					
Black					
Hispanic					
White					
Economic Status:					
Economically Disadvantaged					
Non-Disadvantaged					
Migrant Status					
Migrant					
Non-migrant					

Figure 18. Shell for Table Showing Percentage
of Students Classified as Proficient or Higher,
for Several Possible Cutscores

Cutscore	Cutscore as percent of maximum possible score	Percentage of students classified as Proficient or higher						
		Total	Asian	Black	Hispanic	White	LEP	SWD
24								
23								
22								
21								
20								
19*								
18								
17								
16								
15								
14								

*Cutscore recommended by standard-setting study.

LEP = Limited English Proficiency

SWD = Students with Disabilities

The policymakers need to consider how the results from each
assessment fit into the entire assessment program. In a school
setting, policymakers should compare the distribution of test
takers classified into the same performance levels in different
grades. It would be helpful to provide the comparative
information across grades in a separate table.

Policymakers would be unwise to adopt a set of cutscores that
lead to sharp differences across grade levels in the percent of
students classified as Proficient in a subject, unless there is
good evidence that these differences are real. For example, it
would not be plausible to classify as Proficient 75 percent of the
third graders in a school system, 40 percent of the fourth-
graders, and 70 percent of the fifth-graders. (See section 9,
Consistency Across Grades, for more information on how to
handle unrealistic grade to grade fluctuations.)

In reporting the results of the cutscore study to the policymakers,
you should include information that shows how much the

cutscores of individual participants differed from each other, if the method you used provided cutscores for each participant. Usually, the best way to present this information is in the form of a graph, which enables the policymakers to see at a glance how close the consensus was. We suggest showing the participants' recommended cutscores in a simple bar graph such as the one shown in Figure 19.

Figure 19. Spread of Participants' Cutscores

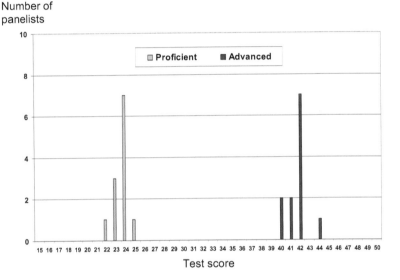

The report of the results of the cutscore study to the policymakers usually includes estimates of the standard error of measurement of the test and of the standard error of judgment of the recommended cutscore.[39] These statistics are based on

---

[39] The *standard error of measurement* of the test is a measure of the extent to which test takers' *scores* would vary over many repeated testings with different questions, scorers, etc. This statistic tends to be different in different parts of the score scale, so it is best to compute it at the cutscore(s). Your statistician can estimate it for you. The *standard error of judgment* is a measure of the extent to which the *cutscore* would vary if the cutscore study were replicated with many different samples of participants. Your statistician can estimate it for you, if you used a method that produces a separate cutscore for each participant.

concepts that are unfamiliar to most people, and policymakers without statistical training need help to interpret them correctly. The "standard error of judgment" is based on the assumption that the participants are a random sample from a very large population of possible participants, which is not likely to be true. It is intended to convey how closely the individual participants agreed, but there are better ways to communicate this information (as described above). In practice, the most common use of these statistics by policymakers has been to provide what appears to be a psychometric rationale for choosing an amount by which to adjust the cutscore.[40]

After considering all the relevant information, the policymakers will have to choose the operational cutscores. That choice is a policy decision, and the policymakers will have to consider the likely consequences of their decision and accept the responsibility for it. We suggest that you encourage the policymakers to provide a rationale for any changes they make to the provisional cutscore, but they are not obligated to provide one. The final operational cutscore should be included in the final documentation.

7.4 Evaluate the Cutscores

The job of setting cutscores is not really completed until the evaluation of the cutscores has been done. Part of the planning and budgeting for a cutscore study should include planning and budgeting for the evaluation phase of the project. You may be evaluating your own cutscores, or an external evaluator may be brought in for that task. In this section, *you* refers to the person in charge of the evaluation.

The job of setting cutscores is not really completed until the evaluation of the cutscores has been done.

We cannot categorize cutscores as right or wrong because the "rightness" of a cutscore is a matter of values and different people hold different values. We do believe, however, that some cutscores are better than others. Some cutscores are

---

[40] We would like to point out that, while use of a standard error as an amount of adjustment to a provisional cutscore appears to have an aura of statistical authority associated with it, there is no scientific reason why it is better than any other reasonable adjustment.

credible, appropriate and useful and some cutscores are inappropriate and counterproductive.

How can you evaluate cutscores? In general, appropriate cutscores have the following characteristics:

- The cutscores were generated by a reasonable method that was implemented in a reasonable way.
- The cutscores were based on the judgments of a representative sample of qualified people.
- The results of using the cutscores are consistent with information obtained from other sources.
- The use of the cutscores helps a testing program meet its goals.

7.4.1 Evaluate the Method and Participants in a Cutscore Study

A cutscore is more likely to be appropriate if it is produced by qualified and well-trained participants using a well-selected and well-run method of setting cutscores, than if it is produced by unqualified participants using a poorly chosen and poorly implemented method.

Therefore, evaluation of the cutscore should begin with evaluation of the cutscore study. Does documentation exist to allow you to evaluate the cutscore study? If not, there is no basis to believe the process contributed to the quality of the cutscore.

If the documentation does exist, was the method selected one that made sense in the circumstances? Was the method implemented in a reasonable way? Were the participants well-trained? Did they evaluate the training favorably?

Is information available about the qualifications of the participants? If not, an important source of evidence is missing and its absence will lower confidence in the cutscores. If the evidence exists, did the participants have the desired qualifications and demographic characteristics? Were they, as a group, representative of all qualified participants? Was there a sufficient number of participants?

Do the performance level descriptors and descriptions of borderline performance (if used) seem clear and complete?

What data were provided to the participants to help them in their task? We think that cutscores based on the judgments of participants who had access to data about real test takers are likely to be more appropriate than cutscores based on judgments made in the absence of such data. Furthermore, we believe the cutscores are likely to be more appropriate if the procedure includes more than one round of judgments and the participants are allowed to discuss their judgments with each other. Considering each other's points of view can help participants reach closer agreement in their judgments. Did the participants have the opportunity to discuss their opinions with each other?

If the participants made judgments about test questions, were those judgments consistent with available data about test takers' actual performance? For example, were borderline test takers judged to perform better on the easier questions than on the harder questions? Consistency with relevant data from other sources is an important attribute of appropriate cutscores.

How closely did the participant's cutscores agree with each other at each round of judgment? If a cutscore method is working appropriately, the judgments of participants should tend to converge as the study progressed. Did that occur?

Did participants evaluate the cutscore study favorably? The evaluations of the participants are not proof of the quality of a cutscore study nor of the cutscores produced, but if the participants do not believe the cutscores that they set are appropriate, neither should you.

7.4.2 Evaluate the Consistency of the Cutscores with What We Know from Other Sources

Important evidence for the usefulness of a cutscore is the extent to which the results of using the cutscore fit with our knowledge about test takers obtained from other sources. Consider the situation in which cutscores are used to classify high school juniors and seniors as Advanced in mathematics. It is useful to look for other indicators of advanced status in mathematics and see if the cutscores are consistent with

Important evidence for the usefulness of a cutscore is the extent to which the results of using the cutscore fit with our knowledge about test takers obtained from other sources.

166

those other indicators. For example, it is reasonable to assume that high school students who score high enough on an Advanced Placement test to qualify for college credit in calculus should be classified as Advanced in mathematics. If many students whose Advanced Placement scores qualify them for college credit in mathematics are classified below the Advanced level, you have strong evidence that the cutscore for the Advanced level is inappropriately high.

Another indicator of advanced status in mathematics would be the grades that students receive in high school math classes. If many students with high grades in honors courses tend not to be classified as Advanced, you have evidence that the Advanced cutscore is too high, assuming the grades are appropriate. Grade inflation is common and may contaminate grades used as an indicator of status in mathematics, or in any other tested subject. If many students with poor grades in mathematics are classified as Advanced by the use of the cutscore, you have evidence that the cutscore is inappropriately low, again assuming that the grades are appropriate.

> *Some authors have suggested using several different methods of setting cutscores and combining their results. We are not comfortable with that suggestion. We prefer to place our resources in one well-selected method and implement it as well as possible...*

Are the pass rates or the proportions of test takers in each performance level generally in line with expectations? For example, what percent of the students in remedial math classes were labeled as Proficient in math on the state's accountability test? If many so-called Proficient students require remediation, there is evidence that the cutscore between Basic and Proficient is inappropriately low.

Some authors have suggested using several different methods of setting cutscores and combining their results. We are not comfortable with that suggestion. We prefer to place our resources in one well-selected method and implement it as well as possible rather than spread our resources across several different methods of setting cutscores.

You can, however, gather information about the appropriateness of a cutscore by conducting an informal

Contrasting Groups study. To do this, have people who know the test takers place them in performance levels without regard to their test scores. For example, in a school setting, you can give teachers the performance level descriptors and ask teachers to identify students they believe are in each performance level *before* you let them know the test scores of the students.

The teachers will not be trained to make the judgments as would the participants in a cutscore study, and the teachers will not have discussions of the intermediate results as would the participants in a cutscore study. Nonetheless, the results of using the cutscores should be generally in line with the classifications made by the teachers. Clear discrepancies can help you identify problems with the cutscores. For example, if very few of the students whom the teachers identified as belonging in the Advanced performance level scored above the cutscore for Advanced, the cutscore may be too high. If many of the students whom the teachers classified as Proficient scored below the cutscore for Basic, that cutscore may be too high.

In an occupational setting, the results of using the cutscore should generally be consistent with previous experience. For example, if almost all of the graduates of a particular training program have been rated acceptable as entry level workers by their supervisors, then almost all of the graduates of that training program should be above the cutscore on a licensing test intended to measure the proficiency of entry level workers (if it is safe to assume that the quality of the people entering the program has not changed). If only about half of the graduates have been rated acceptable as entry level workers, then only about half of the graduates should be above the cutscore on the licensing test, unless the educational program has changed in significant ways.

Also in an occupational setting, assuming no drastic changes in the work over time, most of a sample of qualified practitioners should pass the licensing test. Most of a sample of unqualified people (e.g., people who are similar to the qualified practitioners in many respects but who lack the relevant knowledge and skills) should fail the licensing test. If the qualified practitioners fail, the cutscore is likely to be too high. If the unqualified people pass, the cutscore is likely to be too low. This mode of evaluation is based on the assumptions that the test is a valid measure of the knowledge and skills it is intended to measure and that the determination of who is and who is not a qualified practitioner is made on the basis of the skills the test is intended to measure.

7.4.3 Evaluate the Extent to Which the Cutscores Met Their Purpose

An important aspect of the evaluation of cutscores can be the extent to which the purpose for setting the cutscores is being achieved. Two of the questions we suggested asking policymakers to help them decide whether or not to set cutscores are, "What is the overall objective of using cutscores?" and "How will you know whether or not the objective has been met?" The answers to those questions can help you evaluate the cutscores that were set.

The problem with the criterion of the extent to which the cutscores are meeting their purpose is that appropriate cutscores may not have the intended effects, for many reasons unrelated to the cutscores (e.g., lack of funds, bureaucratic inertia, inappropriate regulations, lack of qualified teachers, lack of experienced school leaders, and so forth). Therefore, failure to meet the objectives of using the cutscores is not necessarily evidence that the cutscores are inappropriate. Success in meeting the objectives, however, can be construed as evidence that use of the cutscores is appropriate.

7.4.4 Summary of Evaluation Requirements

You will never be able to *prove* that a cutscore is appropriate. You should, however, be able to gather evidence about the extent to which the cutscore study was well-chosen to meet the circumstances of the testing program, the extent to which it was implemented as designed, the extent to which the participants were qualified, and the extent to which the results of using the cutscores are consistent with other sources of information. You may also be able to find evidence that the purpose for using the cutscores is being met.

8. TIPS

In this section, we share our experiences in running cutscore studies and provide helpful hints, tips on managing particular challenges, and answers to frequently asked questions.

8.1 Plan the Cutscore Study

Our first tip is that we very strongly recommend making a detailed, written plan for the cutscore study. Here are some of the steps you should consider including in your plan:

- *Obtain staff to carry out the work you cannot do yourself.* A cutscore study requires staff to fill the following roles: a facilitator, a subject-matter expert, a testing expert, a statistician, and a document manager. Large studies may require additional support. Ensure that you have adequate staff on site and others available via telephone or e-mail to provide any information you may need. It is prudent to have a qualified substitute available for each key person.

- *Set dates for the cutscore study.* Most cutscore studies take 2–3 days. The time required will depend on the methodology, the number of tests, the length of the tests, and the number of cutscores that need to be set. Try to avoid conflicts with holidays or popular scheduled events (e.g., major sporting events) that will reduce the pool of potential participants. You should obtain a multi-cultural calendar that shows the major holidays of many religions.

- *Determine any legal requirements for the use of cutscores in your situation.* We recommend that you have your plan for setting cutscores reviewed by a lawyer as soon as possible.

- *Help policymakers decide on the performance levels to use* (e.g., Pass, Fail; Basic, Proficient, Advanced). If you can influence the policymakers, try to have no more performance levels than are necessary to accomplish the goals of using cutscores. Also try to use labels that do not carry excess meaning beyond the knowledge and skills covered by the tests.

- *Review various methods of setting cutscores and select the most appropriate one for your particular circumstances.* Do not limit your choices to the methods discussed in this manual. We did not cover all of the available methods when we wrote the manual, and new methods will continue to be developed after this manual has been published.

- *Decide on the type and timing of data to provide to participants.* Determine whether data such as percent correct values for test questions and impact data should be presented and, if so, when. We strongly recommend the presentation of such data.

- *Prepare an agenda.* The agenda will be specific to the study and will depend on the length of the test, the number of cutscores that must be set, the amount of feedback to be given, the number of iterations of judgments, and the method selected. One of our reviewers suggested adding liberal breaks to the agenda. If something goes wrong, you and your staff will have some extra time to fix the problem. If some tasks take longer than expected, you can reduce the break time to help you remain on schedule. If everything goes well, your participants will appreciate the breaks.

- *Decide on the population of appropriate participants.* The cutscore depends heavily on the judgments of the people who set it. Find out if the policymakers want to specify the qualifications required of participants or if they want the opportunity to approve the targeted qualifications that you specify. The mix of participants has to be acceptable to the various constituencies who have a stake in the outcomes of the cutscore study. For example, if 15% of the people who are qualified to be participants are Hispanic, your mix of participants should include about 15% Hispanic participants.

- *Compile a list of participants to invite to the cutscore study.* The group should be diverse and representative of the entire population of people qualified to be participants. Be prepared to hold several rounds of invitations to meet the specified requirements for the pool of participants.

- *Send a letter of invitation to potential participants.* The letter should explain the importance of participating in the cutscore study, describe the process, state the qualifications required of participants, explain the duties of a participant, clearly state the time commitment, and provide an agenda. Be sure to cover logistics such as transportation, food, lodging, reimbursement for expenses, payment, and so forth. Ask if the participant has any dietary restrictions or needs any accommodations for a disability.

Include your email address and phone number. Indicate that you welcome questions from potential participants.

- *Develop performance level descriptors.* This can be a big job in a K–12 setting because you need a separate performance level descriptor for each performance level, for each subject, for each grade.

- *Obtain data on the test from a sample of test takers.* This step is strongly recommended for all methods and required by some methods. It is very useful to obtain data that allow you to predict the impact or consequences of using the cutscores. The results of using cutscores operationally should not be an unpleasant surprise.

> **It is very useful to obtain data that allow you to predict the impact or consequences of using the cutscores. The results of using cutscores operationally should not be an unpleasant surprise.**

- *Find and reserve space to hold meetings of participants and arrange for transportation, food, and lodging for participants as necessary.* You need meeting space. Ideally, you should use a location away from the participants' work locations to avoid disruptions. The rooms should be spacious and comfortable enough for long discussions. If you are running multiple sessions, you will need one large meeting room for initial introductions and training, and several smaller meeting rooms (which must be large enough to be bearable for several hours) for each session. Decide if you want to seat the participants in a single large group, or in smaller groups at separate tables. Make sure the place where you hold the meetings can provide the kind of seating you desire. You also will need a separate space for lunch and coffee breaks. Having coffee breaks and meals on the same tables that hold the documents used by the participants can be a messy problem.

- *Develop training materials for the participants.* Prepare an introductory presentation that is general enough to use, with only minor revisions, for all the tests in your study. It should focus on the purpose of setting cutscores and on general information about cutscores. Also prepare a separate presentation that is specific to the method that you have chosen. The presentation should guide the participants through the operational steps of the process. These materials should be reviewed by experienced facilitators before you use them.

- *Prepare data entry and statistical calculation software.* Have your statistician program a spreadsheet or other statistical software to calculate cutscores automatically, once the participants' judgments have been entered. The software should also have the capability to calculate all necessary statistical information for the participants, including average judgments, variances in judgments, and the impact of using selected cutscores. See if it is feasible to automate data entry by use of portable scanners.

- *Create practice materials.* Create all the materials the participants will need for the portions of their training sessions in which they practice making their judgments. You should have practice materials available for each subject in which you are setting cutscores. For methods based on judgments about test questions, you will need 15–20 test questions *other* than those on the test itself. Obtain any statistical information you will need about the practice questions (e.g., proportion-correct statistics, or, for the Bookmark or ID Matching methods, IRT difficulty estimates).

- *Develop or obtain the materials required by the method you have chosen.* For example, if you are using the Bookmark or Item Descriptor Matching method, you will have to create the Ordered Item Booklets. If you are using the Angoff or Nedelsky methods, you will need test booklets. For the Analytic Judgment or Body of Work methods, you will need test takers' responses to performance test questions. A sample list of materials is included later in this section.

- *Design recording forms.* For some methods, you will need a form on which the participants can record their judgments. The recording form should be designed to be easy for the participants to use. It should also be compatible with the input requirements of the software you plan to use to help ensure accurate data transfer. You will most likely need separate forms for the practice ratings and for the operational ratings.

- *Design evaluation forms.* We recommend at least three evaluation forms—one to be completed at the end of the training session, one to be completed at the end of Round 1 (to reveal any concerns the participants may have about the operational materials or the judging task, before it is too late to make any adjustments) and one to be completed at the end of the cutscore study. The form should include some yes-no questions and/or some questions with Likert-type scales (e.g., strongly agree, agree, disagree, strongly disagree) that are easy to complete and review. It should also include open questions, in response to which the participants can freely express any concerns or sources of confusion.

- *Write a script or outline.* We recommend that inexperienced facilitators follow a script when running a cutscore study. More experienced facilitators can use a detailed outline. A script or outline is particularly useful to help ensure consistency when two or more facilitators will be working simultaneously. Obviously, not every question can be anticipated, and not every instruction needs to be given verbatim. However, certain pieces, such as the instructions for the judgmental task, should be included and worded as clearly as possible. The script or outline should include directions for displaying the slides and for distributing materials. The script or outline should be circulated and reviewed in advance by all the facilitators to ensure that everyone is in agreement on the steps and how various concepts will be explained. If possible, obtain a review from an experienced facilitator.

- *Train any additional facilitators.* When the cutscore studies involve two or more facilitators, it is important that they all provide the same information to all participants if the cutscore studies are supposed to be comparable. The facilitators have a great deal of power to influence participants' judgments, so it is important that they all give the same directions and provide the same information to the participants.

- *Rehearse.* Even experienced facilitators should rehearse once before running a cutscore study. We recommend scheduling at least two rehearsals for less experienced facilitators. The first rehearsal should occur more than three weeks before the cutscore study, to give the facilitators time to correct any problems that require further familiarity with the materials and study of the script. The second rehearsal should occur a few days before the start of the cutscore study to cover any last minute changes in plans. We recommend having each novice facilitator practice out loud, with an experienced facilitator listening for any problems.

- *Train participants.* The quality and amount of training that you provide to the participants can make or break a cutscore study. The participants may be asked to make difficult and unfamiliar judgments. They may be exposed to new concepts such as borderline performance and response probabilities. Good training and realistic practice sessions are crucial to the success of a cutscore study. Do not skimp on these steps.

> **Good training and realistic practice sessions are crucial to the success of a cutscore study. Do not skimp on these steps.**

- *Set the provisional cutscores.* This is the step in which you actually run the cutscore study. This is when all of the planning pays off. Add allotted times for each activity to your outline or script to help you keep the work on schedule.

- *Compensate participants.* Give the participants a realistic estimate of when their payments and reimbursements for expenses will be made to them, and then make sure that the checks are mailed on schedule. If the participants are teachers and you hold the meetings during school hours, some jurisdictions require you to pay for substitute teachers.

- *Provide information to the policymakers who set the operational cutscores.* Policymakers typically are not familiar with statistical concepts. They tend to have limited amounts of time to devote to cutscores. They appreciate a brief, clear summary of the information they need to select the operational cutscore, with details in an appendix they can relegate to staff.

- *Document the entire process.* You will need complete documentation of what you did, why you did it, and the interim and final results. Sample materials should also be included.

- *Evaluate the cutscores after they have been used.* The process of setting cutscores should include evaluation. The evaluation step should be included in your initial planning to make it more likely that staff and budgets will be available for this crucial task.

As you can see from the list of steps, you should allow plenty of time for getting ready to run the cutscore meeting. One good way to determine when you should begin the work is to count backwards from the time the cutscores must be completed. Some steps can be carried on simultaneously if you have enough staff, but some tasks must be done sequentially. To complicate matters, there are some steps that will not be under your control as a cutscore

> *One good way to determine when you should begin the work is to count backwards from the time the cutscores must be completed.*

facilitator. For example, you will not be able to construct Ordered Item Booklets until you have IRT data for the questions. You cannot get IRT data until the tests have been administered, scored, and calibrated. The tests can not be administered until they have been printed and shipped. The tests can not be printed until development is completed, and so forth. You may have to coordinate your schedule with the test provider to be sure you will have the data and materials you need, when you need them.

The information in this manual should help you estimate how long it will take to prepare for and to complete each step under your control. The entire process of setting cutscores is likely to take longer than you think it will. For example, you may get too few responses to your first request for participants and you may have to send out a second round of invitations. You may not be able to find a time when a sufficient number of participants will be able to meet until far later than you anticipated, and so forth.

If possible, you should leave time in your schedule for a make-up cutscore study because even if everything has been well-planned, problems may occur in execution. Here are some examples of problems we have experienced at various times in various locations: (1) Many of the expected participants simply failed to appear and there were not enough participants to have a credible study. (2) Hotel staff could not locate all of the materials that were shipped to the hotel in advance of the cutscore study. (3) A flood delayed the arrival of most of the participants and much of the first day was lost. (4) Schools closed because of a storm and many of the participants who had children in school had to leave or take time to arrange for child care. (5) The laptop computer containing the slides for the presentations to the participants did not work. (6) Electrical power to the meeting room was cut off for several hours. (7) A facilitator became too ill to continue running the meeting.

In setting a cutscore, as in other areas of life, it is wise to assume that if something can go wrong, it will. It is not unreasonable to allow a full year from the time you begin planning what has to be done to the time that the cutscores are needed.

8.2 Prepare Materials

Here is a list of materials most of which are required for any cutscore study. The materials required for particular methods are indicated.

- Study plan
- Script or outline for facilitator
- Letter of invitation to participants
- Written statement of purpose and brief explanation of the process (consider mailing to participants before the study)
- Agenda (consider mailing to participants before the study)
- Nondisclosure form for secure materials
- Vouchers for reimbursement of travel and other expenses
- Slide show presentations for introduction and training and for running the cutscore study
- Test booklets to familiarize participants with the test and for methods based on judgments of test questions
- Answer key for multiple-choice questions
- Scoring rubrics for constructed-response questions
- Test blueprints/test specifications/content standards
- Performance level descriptors
- Descriptions of borderline performance (unless they will be generated at the meeting)
- Sample of test questions for training participants
- Samples of test takers' performance on constructed-response questions for training participants
- Forms for participants to register complaints about possibly flawed test questions

- Practice materials, such as test questions that are not part of the real test and forms for recording participants' judgments during training exercises
- Evaluation forms for various stages of the cutscore meeting (at least after training, after the first round of judgments, and after the last round of judgments)
- Ordered Item Booklet (for Bookmark and ID Matching methods)
- Item Maps (for Bookmark and ID Matching methods)
- Samples of test takers' performance (for Body of Work, Analytic Judgment, or other Contrasting Groups methods based on evaluations of products)
- Profile Booklets (for Performance Profile Method)
- Operational recording forms for participants' judgments for each round of judgments
- Statistics describing difficulty of test questions
- Statistics describing test performance of groups of students (i.e., impact data)
- Name tags for staff and participants. Identifiers for tables and seating charts for participants
- Pencils and scrap paper for participants
- Sticky notes for use as bookmarks
- Flip charts and markers
- Video/audio playback devices, if necessary for observing samples of test takers' performance
- Calculators for checking computations
- Portable scanner (if used for recording participants' judgments)
- Laptop computer(s), projector and screen for training and display of results
- Laptop computer(s) and software for data entry and the necessary calculations
- Public address system for large or noisy rooms

8.3 Running the Cutscore Study

Be nice to the participants. They are doing you a great favor by attending the meeting. Thank the participants profusely and go out of your way to make them comfortable. Do not do anything to make them angry or annoyed. For example, we have seen a cutscore study get off to a terrible start because the facilitator would not allow the participants to bring their cell phones into the meeting room.[41] We have seen animosity develop in another study because the facilitator gave the impression that he did not trust the participants to handle secure test materials.

Treat the participants as professionals and try to respond to all of their questions and requests for information. Do not imply that anything related to the test or to the cutscore setting process is too esoteric for the participants to understand. It is your responsibility to have comprehensible answers to the participants' questions, or to have experts available who can provide such answers.

> *Treat the participants as professionals and try to respond to all of their questions and requests for information.*

Keep communications open among staff so that participants are not getting mixed messages. This is particularly important if the study involves two or more groups working separately. For example, if a problem arises for one group, that problem and the way it was handled should be communicated to the facilitators working with the other groups.

If a participant asks a question that you do not know how to answer, tell the participants you will get that information for them. Then delegate someone to find the answer. If the question is a policy question, it may need to be answered by a policymaker. If it is a statistical question, it may need to be answered by a statistician. It is important to arrange to have knowledgeable people either on site or available quickly by telephone or e-mail to answer questions.

---

[41] We recommend allowing participants to keep their cell phones. Just ask the participants not to use the phones in the room where confidential materials are exposed.

8.4 Common Problems and Suggested Solutions

There are common problems that arise in almost any cutscore study. No matter how well prepared you are, you are likely to face problems with performance level descriptors, management of the cutscore study, test questions, calculations and data, and participants.

8.4.1 Performance Level Descriptors

There are two primary problems in working with performance level descriptors during a cutscore study. The first problem is that participants may not all have the same interpretation of the meaning of the performance level descriptors. The second problem is that participants may want to change the meaning of the performance level descriptors. (If it is the participants' responsibility to write the performance level descriptors, this is not a problem. Usually, however, performance level descriptors are established before the cutscore meeting and should not be changed at the cutscore meeting.)

It is very important that you ensure that all participants are in agreement on the meaning of the performance level descriptors before proceeding. It is necessary for participants to share a common understanding of the performance level descriptor, or they will never come to any type of agreement on the cutscore for meeting that descriptor. Focus the group discussion on the examples of what test takers who just meet each descriptor can and cannot do. If there is disagreement, identify the specific points of disagreement and ask the participants to work together to come to an agreement about what behaviors would be considered examples of each level of performance. It is important that participants understand that there will be a range of skills within each level. Not all Proficient test takers will have exactly the same knowledge and skills. That is, a barely Proficient test taker will have a different level of knowledge and skills than a highly Proficient (but not yet Advanced) test taker.

We suggest beginning with the most important distinction between performance levels. For example, for NCLB the most important distinction is between Basic and Proficient. Focus on what distinguishes the lowest Proficient performance from the highest Basic performance (i.e., borderline Proficient knowledge and skills). Ask questions such as, "What can the barely Proficient test taker do that the highest performing Basic test taker cannot do?" Then focus on the lowest Advanced performance and the highest Proficient performance (i.e., borderline Advanced knowledge and skills.) By specifying the borders between each pair of adjacent performance levels, you will clarify the range of performance within each performance level.

At times in the discussion of the borderline test taker, participants want to change the performance level descriptor. Unless the participants are responsible for writing the performance level descriptors, any changes to the descriptors should be limited to clarifications of knowledge and skills already included, rather than the addition or the removal of any knowledge or skills.

To help clarify the task, we typically ask the participants to think in terms of behaviors a borderline test taker might exhibit. For example, if borderline test takers have a basic understanding of simple algebraic concepts, what types of problems/tasks will they be able to do? What types will they struggle with? Focusing on behaviors allows participants to create a fine-grained description of the borderline test taker without changing the meaning of the original performance level descriptor. We suggest that you or someone you designate act as a note taker and post the results of the participants' deliberations about borderline behavior for all to see.

Some methods, such as the Bookmark, include a step at the end of the cutscore study in which participants review the questions falling in each performance level and modify the performance level descriptor accordingly. Again, these modifications should only be clarifications, or additions of detail, not outright changes. If the policymakers have approved the performance level descriptors before the cutscore study, the meaning of the descriptors should not be changed. We encourage participants to add descriptions that would make the requirements of each level clearer to the test taker, the teacher, the score user, or other stakeholders, but not to alter the meaning of any descriptor.

8.4.2 Management

It is very important to have the right staff on site and to be sure that each staff member is clear about his or her responsibilities. We recommend giving all staff members a written statement of who is responsible for each activity that must be carried out, and when in the agenda that activity is likely to arise.

We suggest that you designate one room as the "office" where you keep all secure materials, post updated information for the staff, and hold staff meetings. If you are running your cutscore study in a hotel, this means renting an extra room, but we have found it is well worth the money. We often use this room for all data entry tasks and calculations, so that we can talk about the data without influencing the participants. It is also useful to have a place where you and your colleagues can talk freely (and privately) about problems with particular participants.

Security is a concern with most tests. Having a separate office at the site allows you to keep the materials in a locked location that is less likely to be disturbed than is a meeting room. (We have had several experiences with cleaning staff at a hotel unlocking a meeting room and leaving it unlocked in spite of assurances from the hotel management that the room would be undisturbed.) We also recommend numbering each copy of each secure document and keeping track of which participant has been given each copy. Secure documents should never be left unattended in an unlocked room. When the participants leave for lunch or breaks, either assign a staff member to guard the room, or lock the room. All secure materials should be checked back in before the participants leave for the day. We also recommend printing all secure material on colored paper so that it becomes easier to keep track of it among all the papers used in a cutscore study.

8.4.3 Test Questions

You should expect participants to criticize some of the test questions. Unsolicited review of test questions is a very common occurrence at cutscore meetings. If you try to prevent it, you will frustrate and anger the participants. You will need to allow the participants to express their opinions about the test questions without allowing the cutscore meeting to become a test evaluation meeting.

You will need to allow the participants to express their opinions about the test questions without allowing the cutscore meeting to become a test evaluation meeting.

We believe that the best strategy is to build some time into the agenda for review of the test questions, the test blueprints, the test specifications, and/or the content standards. We also recommend that you allow time for some discussion of the questions. We usually allow 20 or so minutes for criticism of the questions, after the participants have finished taking or reviewing the test. Many methods of setting cutscores include a careful review of what each question is measuring, but this additional discussion allows the participants to voice their concerns about "problems" with the questions and remain on schedule.

If the discussion is lasting too long, tell the participants that their concerns and opinions are very important, but the purpose of the cutscore study is to set a cutscore, not to evaluate the questions. Explain that there is a lot of work to do and that it is important to follow the agenda or the main task will not be completed. Then suggest that the participants put their concerns about the questions in writing, clearly specifying the test, the question number, and the problem, so that you can communicate their concerns to the appropriate person. Once you have made such a promise, you must follow through and deliver the comments to someone responsible for the development of the test. The goal is to allow the participants' to express their concerns about the questions to the test developers while you maintain a focus on setting cutscores. Tell the participants not to expect to hear directly from the test developers unless you have made arrangements to obtain responses to the participants' comments from the test developers.

Occasionally, the participants do find a truly flawed question, such as a question that has been keyed incorrectly or a multiple-choice question with two correct answers. If a question is clearly flawed, the best strategy is to tell participants to ignore the question when they make their judgments about cutscores. If, however, the criticized question is not clearly flawed, tell the participants to respond to the question as it is when they make their cutscore-related judgments.

Participants in a Bookmark study often disagree with the ordering of the questions. They might think that some questions toward the back of the Ordered Item Booklet (e.g., those that statistically are the most difficult) are easier than some of the questions that were placed earlier in the Booklet. First, check to be sure that the Booklets were assembled correctly. If they are correct, explain that the order of the questions is based on test takers' actual responses to the questions. If the participants believe a question is misplaced, they should look for features of the question that could have made it harder or easier than it seems. Also remind the participants that a question at the end of the test may be more difficult than it would have been if it had been placed earlier in the test, due to fatigue and timing effects. We recommend always including information on the original question order in the Item Map and telling participants to consider that information in their judgments. See section 6.6 on the Bookmark method for more information on how to work with "out-of-order" questions.

8.4.4 Calculations

You should be absolutely sure to check the accuracy of all quantitative work. Make sure the correct numbers have been entered into the calculations. Make sure the calculations are correct. Make sure the results are correctly reported. There are lots of numbers in a cutscore study. It is very easy to get some of them wrong. For example, an Angoff study with 20 participants, 100 questions, two cutscores, and three rounds of judgments will result in 12,000 numbers that have to be taken from the participants' forms and entered into your computer correctly. To make matters worse, the quantitative work is often done under time pressure while the participants are at lunch or on a break.

> ...*check the accuracy of all quantitative work. Make sure the correct numbers have been entered into the calculations. Make sure the calculations are correct. Make sure the results are correctly reported.*

You must have a quality control process as part of the data entry and for all calculations. For example, if a staff member enters judgments or other data into the computer, a second staff member should check the numbers to be sure they were entered accurately, before any calculations are done. If you use scanners to enter the data, check the results for some selected participants by hand to be sure that the scanners are working correctly. Verify one or two instances of each calculation by hand to make sure the software is working correctly. For example, if software is used to identify the lowest and highest Angoff judgments for a question, a staff member should check a few of the values for consistency with the original entries on the rating forms.

8.4.5 Statistical Information

How much information should you give to participants about the calculations that will convert their individual judgments to a cutscore? The problem is that some participants are confused by an explanation of the trimmed mean in an Angoff study, while other participants demand to know the details of Item Response Theory in a Bookmark study, or exactly how score equating is done.

Our recommendation is to prepare a relatively simple explanation for each important concept, but to be prepared to give more information, including formulas, if the participants ask for them. Your statistician should be prepared to meet, during a break or a meal, with the participants who want detailed quantitative explanations. Consider preparing handouts before the meeting about topics that may puzzle participants, such as Item Response Theory and equating.

It is important to make sure the participants correctly interpret the data you share with them. For example, participants often express frustration when we first show them the percent correct values (p-values) for the questions. We have often heard, "Well, if you already know the probabilities, then why are you wasting our time making us guess them?" It is important to emphasize that the p-values you are giving the participants indicate the percentage of *all* test takers who answered the question correctly, while the participants' task is to estimate the percentage of *borderline* test takers who would answer the question correctly. We expect these numbers to be different.

Often the next question is, "Should my numbers be higher or lower than the p-values?" That is a more difficult question to answer, as it depends on whether the participant thinks the borderline test taker is more or less competent than the average test taker. The answer will certainly depend on which performance level is being judged. For example, the borderline Advanced test takers are highly likely to be more competent than the average test takers. The Below Basic test takers are likely to be less competent than the average test takers.

We also encourage participants to pay attention to *relative* difficulties rather than absolute difficulties. For example, if all test takers did better on question 10 than on question 12, it would probably make sense to expect the Angoff ratings for the borderline students to be higher on question 10 than on question 12.

We also face the question of how much weight participants should give to each type of information we give them. In one cutscore study, a participant said to one of us, "You've told me how my ratings compare to everyone else's ratings, what the p-values are for each question, what my cutscore is, what the average cutscore is, and what percentage of students will pass given the average cutscore. Which piece of information should I use to adjust my ratings?"

Faced with such a question, we encourage the participants to focus on the knowledge and skills required to answer the question correctly compared to the knowledge and skills in the performance level descriptor. The other information is supplementary. We ask the participants to listen to their colleagues with an open mind, but not to be unduly influenced or feel coerced to change their rating. Normative data such as p-values and impact data are supposed to be reality checks. The data are to help the participants make better judgments. The data are not supposed to replace the participants' judgments.

8.4.6 Problem Participants

There are times when a participant must leave before the cutscore study is completed. To minimize this occurrence, inform the participants when they are invited of the duration of the cutscore study and that they are expected to stay through to the end of the study. However, family emergencies or health problems can arise, causing a participant to leave before the end of the cutscore study. Because we know such things happen, we recommend that you invite more participants than are needed to complete the cutscore study. As soon as you know that a participant will be leaving early, you should remove that participant's data from all calculations not yet completed.

Occasionally we encounter uncooperative participants—people who arrive at the cutscore study unwilling to apply a cutscore methodology. For example, one of us encountered a participant who walked into the meeting, stated that all tests are inherently evil, placed his bookmark on the first question, and announced that he was finished. No amount of training or discussion convinced him to review the questions and engage in the

186

Bookmark method. Some participants may be openly hostile and challenge the test and the process of setting cutscores.

> **Establish procedures for dealing with uncooperative or hostile participants _before_ the situation actually arises.**

Establish procedures for dealing with uncooperative or hostile participants <u>before</u> the situation actually arises. Some policymakers may wish to be consulted before you take any such action. Find out before the meeting how much involvement policymakers want in dealing with disruptive participants. You should know in advance who has to approve the decision to remove a participant. You should have rules in place for deciding when to ask a participant to leave, and when to allow a participant to stay but remove that participant's judgments from the final calculation.

In K–12 settings, cutscore studies may double as professional development workshops for the teachers who are participating. Therefore, state policymakers are often reluctant to "fire" a participant. They are also concerned with the bad publicity that a fired participant might cause. However, if a participant is disruptive, you may have to remove the participant from the cutscore study. In our experience, the removal of a participant is exceedingly rare. Only one of us has ever had to remove a disruptive participant. We have found that often the other participants in the group help to calm a disruptive participant.

If the participant is not being disruptive, then it is usually best to allow the participant to stay. If, however, the participant is purposefully not following the procedures (for example, placing a bookmark on the first question, or providing an Angoff rating of 0.25 for every question), then it may be necessary to exclude the participant's judgments from the data used to calculate the cutscore. You should establish clear guidelines in advance of the study for deciding whether a participant's data should be discarded.

If a participant is following directions but simply has a different opinion from the other participants, that participant's judgments should not be excluded from the cutscore calculations. A participant's judgments should be excluded from the calculations only if the participant is clearly violating the procedures of the cutscore study. Before excluding a participant's judgments from the calculations, give the participant every opportunity to take part in the cutscore study. Explain how the judgments will be used, clarify any instructions necessary, and point out that the best way to influence a decision is to participate fully in the process.

We believe that the best strategy is to use the median or the trimmed mean to find the average of the cutscores implied by the participant's individual judgments. In that way, extreme opinions will automatically be removed and you will not have to take specific action against any participant. Be sure to tell participants what averaging method you will be using before you begin to collect their judgments.

8.4.7 Questions Frequently Asked by Participants

It is important to distinguish between hostile participants and befuddled participants. Sometimes participants simply need additional instruction or practice to understand what is being asked of them. Here is a list of questions that participants often ask in cutscore studies with the answers that we have found work well. Issues with particular methodologies have been included in sections 4 and 6.

Q: *How much weight will our recommendations carry in determining the final cut scores?*

A: (We suggest that, before the cutscore study, you obtain the answer to this question from the policymakers who will set the operational cutscores. In the absence of a specific response from a policymaker, use the following explanation.) It varies. Some policymakers tend to accept the recommendations with few, if any, changes. Others may make more substantial adjustments. The bottom line is that your cutscore acts as a starting point. The cutscore may be adjusted up or down from your recommendation, but the discussions of the policymakers always take your recommendations as a starting point.

Q: *While I am making the cutscore judgments, if I find a question that I believe should not be on the test or I think it is flawed, what should I do?*

A: (If the content experts have not decided that the question is clearly flawed and should be ignored, and the time allotted for group discussion of the questions has passed, use this response.)The questions on the test have all been developed and reviewed by content experts, but it is possible that you may come across a question that you believe should not be on the test. You will be provided with paper to note your concerns and these will be shared with the appropriate test development experts. But we still need your judgments for those questions. You should consider the "flaws" in the question when making your judgments, especially if those flaws make the question easier or more difficult for a borderline test taker.

Q: *Why are we wasting time discussing what it means to be proficient? Doesn't everyone know what "proficient" means?*

A: Actually, "proficient" has different meanings to different people. For example, some people have defined proficiency as "satisfactory knowledge" while others define it as "mastery over all grade-level material," and yet others define it as "mastery of challenging material." These definitions imply that different people require different levels of knowledge and skills for proficiency. It is important to ensure that everyone participating in setting cutscores on this test is thinking about the same requirements for proficiency.

8.4.8 Defusing Arguments Among Groups of Participants

One disadvantage of seating the participants in small groups is that it may exacerbate disagreements among the groups. For example, at one study the participants were divided into two tables. At each table, the participants worked well together and converged nicely on a cutscore recommendation. However, the cutscores differed greatly between the two tables. When we tried to explore the differences in opinions, the discussion quickly broke down into accusations and name calling across the tables.

To resolve this issue, we immediately stopped the discussion and called for a break. While the participants were gone, we reorganized the room, creating one large circle of chairs with no tables. When the participants returned, we asked them to take a seat and purposely intermingled the two groups. We then went around the circle and had the participants each describe the thought processes they went through in deciding on a cut score. The new configuration helped alter the us-versus-them mentality and turned the discussion into a productive exchange of thoughts and ideas. The problem of "taking sides" is not common enough to override the benefits that usually follow from the ease of discussion when the participants are grouped at separate tables. It is useful, however, to be aware of the remedy if the problem does occur during your study.

8.4.9 Special Populations of Test Takers

The *No Child Left Behind* legislation has increased the focus on testing all students, including those who do not speak English well and those with disabilities. In most cases, these students take the same test that most other students take, but they are given accommodations in accordance with their special needs. However, a small percentage of the population with the most significant cognitive disabilities may be assessed with a separate test and evaluated against alternate achievement standards. These alternate assessments often differ significantly from the assessments used with the other test takers. The alternate assessments may consist of a checklist of skills that an instructor completes, a portfolio of work reflecting indicators most relevant to each individual, or a small set of performance tasks.

The same number of cutscores (typically 2–3) may need to be set on these assessments as on the general assessments. One concern is that these assessments often have a much smaller point range and thus cannot support multiple cutscores well. Another concern is that the number of test takers may be so small that there are gaps in the score distribution. The gaps may reduce the amount of data you can use to help set reasonable cutscores. However, overall, the task of setting cutscores on these alternate measures does not differ significantly from the steps described so far in this manual. It is crucial to develop strong performance level descriptors that are applicable to the target population.

For this population, a cutscore methodology focusing on an examination of student work or student abilities is particularly appropriate. Therefore we recommend a method in the Contrasting Groups family of methods. Because the students with significant cognitive disabilities are such a small proportion of the population, it is not as costly to gather opinions on student performance from their teachers as it can be for a regular large-scale assessment. For this population, it is often appropriate to have participants evaluate videotapes of student performance.

190

8.4.10 Exceptions to Decision Rules

We defined cutscores as decision rules and we expressed our opinion that decision rules had advantages over case-by-case decision making. We recommend, however, that you set up a mechanism for allowing exceptions to the decision rules because there may be good reasons for doing so.

> **If you are a policymaker and you decide not to allow any exceptions, you may be forced to make a decision that is unreasonable in some particular case.**

If you are a policymaker and you decide not to allow any exceptions, you may be forced to make a decision that is unreasonable in some particular case. For example, a test taker may have an atypical problem, unrelated to the knowledge and skills being tested, that causes her to get a lower score than other test takers with the same level of knowledge and skills would get. You may believe that it would be appropriate to make an exception to your decision rule for that test taker.

If you could anticipate all the possible reasons that would justify such an exception, you could write them into the decision rule. Unfortunately, no human being can foresee all the possible circumstances in which a decision rule would be unreasonable.

The problem with allowing exceptions is that once you have made an exception, where do you stop? You may find yourself pressured by people seeking exceptions for reasons you do not consider legitimate. Also, exceptions tend to undermine people's faith in the fairness of your decision procedure. An exception that some people regard as fair may look to others like favoritism.

One way to deal with this problem is to have an established procedure for determining whether an exception should be allowed. You might form a standing committee to approve or deny requests for exceptions. If you find a particular type of special circumstance occurring frequently, you can modify your decision rule to cover it. Each time you modify the decision rule in this way, you will reduce the number of exceptions you will have to deal with in the future.

9. CONSISTENCY ACROSS GRADES

At the time that the original *Passing Scores* was written, cutscores were typically used for pass-fail decisions on licensing tests and tests for high school graduation. There was a single pass-fail decision on a test that did not have to be coordinated with other tests. Now, cutscores are widely used to place students into three or more performance levels on tests of reading and math in grades 3 to 8. This expansion in the use of multiple cutscores leads to some new questions: Do the cutscores make sense together? Are the cutscores aligned across grades, subjects, and performance levels in ways that are compatible with reasonable expectations?

If the content standards and performance level descriptors are not properly aligned, the cutscores based on them will not be properly aligned.

"Alignment" generally implies two kinds of relationships: (1) Within each grade, there are reasonable differences between the degrees of knowledge and skills represented by the cutscores for different proficiency levels. (2) The degrees of knowledge and skills represented by the cutscores for the same performance level across grades increase in reasonable ways from one grade to the next. If the content standards and performance level descriptors are not properly aligned, the cutscores based on them will not be properly aligned.

If the test scores are "vertically scaled" for comparability of scores across grade levels within a subject,[42] the cutscores should increase as the grade levels increase. For example, the cutscore for Proficient in grade 7 should be higher than the cutscore for Proficient in grade 6. If the test scores are not vertically scaled, the scores should not be compared across grades.

---

[42] In a vertical scale a single score scale is used across several grade levels. For example, vertically scaled scores of 300 on the 4th-grade and 5th-grade tests in the same subject indicate the same level of knowledge and skill, if the skills tested at the two grade levels are similar. However, the level of proficiency represented by a score of 300 may be considered Advanced for fourth-graders but merely Proficient for fifth-graders.

Whether or not a vertical scale is used, large, unanticipated differences across grades in the percentages of students in the various performance levels are cause for concern. Unless there is evidence to indicate that these differences are real, they imply a problem with one or more of the cutscores. It is not realistic to expect the percentages to remain the same in all the grades or to change by the same amount at every grade level. But it is realistic to expect that the percent of test takers within a performance level will not fluctuate sharply from grade to grade with no reason. In short, the percentages of students in the performance levels should make sense and fit with reality. For example, if the percentages of students classified as Proficient or above in math in grades 3 to 8 are 72, 79, 54, 81, 85, and 83, respectively, it is wise to investigate the reasons for the low percentage in grade 5. If there are no reasons to explain such a drop, it is likely that the cutscore for Proficient in grade 5 is inappropriately high.

> *It is not realistic to expect the percentages to remain the same in all the grades or to change by the same amount at every grade level. But it is realistic to expect that the percent of test takers within a performance level will not fluctuate sharply from grade to grade with no reason.*

Understanding the nature of alignment is important. Alignment does not require that the percentages of students at a given performance level in a particular subject area be even roughly the same across all grades. Though roughly equal percentages across grades may occur, other patterns are possible. As an example, consider a typical school accountability measure: the percentage of students scoring at or above the Proficient level. As the content becomes more difficult in higher grades, the percentages might decrease from grade 3 to grade 8. On the other hand, as teachers have both the information and the incentive to focus their instruction on students below the Proficient level, greater percentages of students might reach Proficient or above in the later grades than in the earlier grades. Any of these patterns of results might occur. Sharp grade to grade fluctuations are likely to signal problems with the cutscores, however, in the absence of plausible explanations for the differences.

What should you do if the percentages indicate that the cutscores are poorly aligned? You might decide to do nothing. This option has the advantage of being quick and effortless. Furthermore it carries no taint of "rigging" the results to make them come out in any particular way. It places full trust in the participants who set the cutscores at the various grade-levels. The disadvantage, of course, is that it does nothing to correct inappropriate, unjustified differences in the impact of using the cutscores.

If you believe that consistency across grades is important, then you should use procedures that are likely to result in alignment. We will describe several options and what we believe to be the advantages and disadvantages of each, but we cannot yet make recommendations based on either research or personal experience.

If the cutscores have not yet been set, you can sequence the cutscore meetings to allow results of the earlier meetings to influence the participants in the later meetings. For example, start with grades 5 and 6. Then share the grade 5 outcomes with the grade 4 panel and the grade 6 outcomes with the grade 7 panel, and so forth. The advantage of these procedures is that you are depending on the participants' judgments and providing them with relevant information. There is no taint of "rigging" the outcomes. You will, however, have to train the participants to use the additional data. A disadvantage of this approach is the earliest meetings have the greatest influence on the full set of cutscores. Decisions made at the earlier meetings will influence the later meetings, but decisions made at the later meetings can not influence the earlier meetings. An inappropriately high (or low) cutscore chosen at an early meeting—especially at the first meeting—will tend to produce inappropriately high (or low) cutscores at all the later meetings.

An option that avoids the disadvantage of overly weighting decisions made at the earlier meetings is to run the cutscore meetings simultaneously. Have representatives from each meeting gather together for discussion of their results after each major stage of cutscore setting. For example, the representatives could meet after borderline performance has been defined to ensure that the definitions are aligned. They could meet after each round of judgments to help attain alignment, and they could meet after the provisional cutscores have been set to make any necessary additional adjustments. There is no taint of "rigging" the outcome because you are depending on the participants' judgments. The disadvantage of this option is that it extends the time required for the cutscore meetings and complicates the procedures by adding more information to be assimilated and more steps to be followed.

For all of the following options, you will need data that your statistician can use to calculate the impact of setting cutscores at various points. The statistician will need to calculate the percent of students classified into each performance level by a given set of cutscores. The statistician will also need to calculate the cutscores that will place, as nearly as possible, specified percentages of students into each performance level.

If the cutscores have already been submitted to the policymaker, one option that the policymaker can implement is to revise the cutscores to reduce or eliminate anomalies. This solution is quick and it can correct anomalies. The disadvantages are that policy decisions depend on the subjective judgments of a few people (sometimes as few as one), carry the taint of manipulating the outcome, and may lower confidence in the results. For these reasons, the policymaker may prefer to appoint a separate alignment panel to determine the operational cutscores. The judgments will then be those of a panel of specially qualified people, rather than the decision of a policymaker who may have less expertise in the field. The disadvantages of using an alignment panel are the time and expense of an additional meeting.

You will need to provide appropriate information to the people involved in alignment decisions to help guide their decisions. They should know how the initial cutscores were determined (i.e., the methodology used), where the cutscores were placed, and the projected percentage of students reaching each level of performance. Your statistician should prepare data tables showing the percentages of students in each grade who are at each performance level, for each plausible cutscore.

One way to adjust cutscores that produce large grade to grade fluctuations is to apply a smoothing procedure to the percentages of students reaching the cutscores at the successive grade levels and then choose the cutscores that come closest to producing the smoothed percentages.

Smoothing adjusts the percentage for each individual grade level on the basis of information from other grade levels.

The implicit assumption is that this percentage will change gradually, not abruptly, from one grade level to the next. (We discussed several smoothing techniques when we described the Contrasting Groups method.) If you state in advance that you will use this procedure to align the cutscores across grades, you are less likely to be accused of manipulating the results.

Another way to avoid grade-to-grade inconsistencies is to set cutscores only at some selected grades rather than at all of the grades in which cutscores are needed. Then choose the cutscores for the other grades by interpolating values for the percent of students reaching the cutscore. For example, you could do cutscore studies at grades 3, 5, 7, and 8. If the results for those grades are acceptable, you could then interpolate the percentages in each performance level to determine the cutscores for grades 4 and 6. Your statistician may decide to interpolate by fitting a smooth curve to the data points rather than using linear interpolation.

> *Smoothing adjusts the percentage for each individual grade level on the basis of information from other grade levels. The implicit assumption is that this percentage will change gradually, not abruptly, from one grade level to the next. If you state in advance that you will use this procedure to align the cutscores across grades, you are less likely to be accused of manipulating the results.*

This approach allows you to reduce the number of cutscore studies that you will have to run. It is particularly useful if satisfactory cutscores for several grades are already in place and cutscores for other grades have to be set. This approach guarantees that there will be no anomalous results for the interpolated grades. It has some disadvantages, however. The results from this approach depend entirely on the cutscore studies at only some of the grade levels. If one of those studies is anomalous in some way, the results at other grade levels will be affected. Another disadvantage is that the cutscores at some grades are determined entirely by participants in cutscore studies at other grades.

Finally, you can combine some of the options such as allowing earlier cutscore studies to influence the later ones and using an alignment panel to adjust any remaining anomalies. Vertical alignment is a relatively new concern and little research exists at this time to guide practice.

10. CONCLUSION

We were limited by our incomplete knowledge and influenced by our subjective likes and dislikes in selecting the methods of setting cutscores to include in this manual. Please do not infer that a method is inappropriate simply because we did not include it. Similarly, do not infer that the specific procedures we recommend for conducting any cutscore study are the only correct procedures.

No matter what method is used to set cutscores, cutscores will always be based on the judgments of some people. Because the cutscores can have important consequences, you should choose those people carefully and train them well in an appropriate method of setting cutscores. You should give the people relevant data to help them make reasonable decisions. You should evaluate the results of using the cutscores, and be willing to revise the cutscores if the benefits of using the cutscores are outweighed by the negative consequences.

> *The process of setting a cutscore can be only as good as the judgments that go into it.*

The process of setting a cutscore can be only as good as the judgments that go into it. The cutscore will depend on whose judgments are involved in the process and on the method that you use to set cutscores. In this sense, all cutscores are subjective. Yet, once a cutscore has been set, the decisions based on it can be made objectively. Instead of a separate set of judgments for each test taker, you will have the same set of judgments applied to all test takers. Cutscores cannot be objectively determined, but they can be objectively applied.

We would like to close with a quotation by Robert Ebel (1972, p. 496) for you to keep in mind as you set cutscores.

> Anyone who expects to discover the "real"
> passing score by any of these approaches,
> or any other approach, is doomed to
> disappointment, for a "real" passing score
> does not exist to be discovered. All any
> examining authority that must set passing scores
> can hope for, and all any of their examinees can
> ask, is that the basis for defining the passing
> score be defined clearly, and that the definition
> be as rational as possible.

Thank you for reading our manual. We hope it will help you set appropriate and useful cutscores.

SUGGESTIONS FOR FURTHER READING

This is not a scholarly bibliography, but simply a list of sources to help you learn more about cutscores than we could include in this manual.

We recommend that you start with the following summary chapters. They include a lot of useful information in relatively few pages.

Cizek, G. J. (2006). Standard setting. In S. M. Downing and T. M. Haladyna (Eds.), *Handbook of test development.* Mahwah, NJ: Erlbaum.

Hambleton, R. K., & Pitoniak, M. J. (2006). Setting performance standards. In R.L. Brennan (Ed.), *Educational measurement* (fourth edition). Westport, CT: Praeger.

If you want more information, we suggest the following books, which are devoted to the issues associated with setting cutscores and the methods for doing so.

Cizek, G. J. (Ed.). (2001). *Setting performance standards: Concepts, methods, and perspectives.* Mahwah, NJ: Erlbaum.

Cizek, G. J., & Bunch, M. B. (2007). *Standard setting: A guide to establishing and evaluating performance standards on tests.* Thousand Oaks, CA: Sage.

If you want even more detail and more background information, pick and choose among the following sources, or use the references cited in the books and chapters listed above. Some of the references below are primarily of historical interest, such as the original description of what came to be known as the Angoff method. We included only published books and journals because the papers delivered at professional conferences can be hard to obtain. If the subject of a document is not clear from the title, we have included a brief note to help you determine whether or not you would be interested in the document.

American Educational Research Association, American Psychological Association, & National Council on Measurement in Education (1999). *Standards for educational and psychological testing*. Washington, DC: American Educational Research Association.

Angoff, W. H. (1971). Scales, norms, and equivalent scores. In R. L. Thorndike (Ed.), *Educational measurement* (second edition, pp. 508–600). Washington, DC: American Council on Education. (For the original description of the Angoff method, see the footnote on p. 515 and the associated text.) This document is available online at: http://www.ets.org/research/researcher/ANG-SCORES.html

Beuk, C. H. (1984). A method for reaching a compromise between absolute and relative standards in examinations. *Journal of Educational Measurement, 21*, 147–152.

Brandon, P. (2004). Conclusions about frequently studied modified Angoff topics. *Applied Measurement in Education, 17*(1).

Breyer, F. J. (1993). The Beuk compromise adjustment: Possible Rx for troubled cut-score study results. *CLEAR Exam Review, IV*, 23–27.

Cizek, G. J. (1996a). Setting passing scores [instructional module from the National Council on Measurement in Education]. *Educational Measurement: Issues and Practice, 15*(2), 20–31.

Cizek, G. J. (1996b). Standard-setting guidelines. *Educational Measurement: Issues and Practice, 15*(1), 13–21, 12.

Cizek, G. J., Bunch, M. B., & Koons, H. (2004). An NCME Instructional Module on Setting Performance Standards: Contemporary Methods. *Educational Measurement: Issues and Practice, 23*(4), 31–50.

Cizek, G. (Ed.). (2005). [Special issue on vertical moderation]. *Applied Measurement in Education, 18*(1).

De Gruijter, D. N. M. (1985). Compromise models for establishing examination standards. *Journal of Educational Measurement, 22,* 263–269.

Ebel, R. L. (1972). *Essentials of educational measurement* (2nd ed.). Englewood Cliffs, NJ: Prentice-Hall. (The original description of the Ebel method and a good introduction to many measurement concepts.)

Hambleton, R. K., Brennan, R. L., Brown, W., Dodd, B., Forsyth, R. A., Mehrens, W. A., et al. (2000). A response to "Setting reasonable and useful performance standards" in the National Academy of Sciences' *Grading the nation's report card. Educational Measurement: Issues and Practice, 19*(2), 5–14. (A defense of methods of setting cutscores based on judgments of test questions, in reply to the paper by Shepard and others cited below.)

Hambleton, R. K., & Plake, B. S. (1995). Extended Angoff procedures to set standards on complex performance assessments. *Applied Measurement in Education, 8,* 41–56.

Hofstee, W. K. B. (1983). The case for compromise in educational selection and grading. In S. B. Anderson and J. S. Helmick (Eds.), *On educational testing.* (pp. 109–127). Washington, DC: Jossey-Bass.

Impara, J. C., & Plake, B. S. (1997). Standard setting: An alternative approach. *Journal of Educational Measurement, 34*(4), 353–366.

Impara, J. C., & Plake, B. S. (Eds.). (1995). Standard setting for complex performance tasks [special issue]. *Applied Measurement in Education, 8*(1).

Jaeger, R. M. (1989). Certification of student competence. In R. Linn (Ed.), *Educational measurement* (third edition, pp. 485–514). Englewood Cliffs, NJ: Prentice-Hall. (A summary chapter about cutscores, the predecessor of the Hambleton and Pitoniak [2006] chapter cited above.)

Jaeger, R. M. (1991). Selection of judges for standard-setting. *Educational Measurement: Issues and Practice, 10*(2), 3–6, 10, 14.

Kane, M. (1998). Choosing between examinee-centered and test-centered standard-setting methods. *Educational Assessment, 5*(3), 129–145.

Kane, M. (1994). Validating the performance standards associated with passing scores. *Review of Educational Research, 64,* 425–461.

Karantonis, A. & Sireci, S. (2006). The bookmark standard-setting method: A literature review. *Educational Measurement: Issues and Practice, 25,* 4–12.

Kingston, N. M., Kahl, S. R., Sweeney, K. P., & Bay, L. (2001). Setting performance standards using the body of work method. In G.J. Cizek (Ed.), *Setting performance standards: Concepts, methods, and perspectives.* Mahwah, NJ: Lawrence Erlbaum Associates.

Livingston, S. A. (1980). Choosing minimum passing scores by stochastic approximation techniques. *Educational and Psychological Measurement, 40*(4), pp. 859–873. (Includes a detailed presentation of the Up and Down method.)

Livingston, S. A. (2004). *Equating test scores (without IRT).* Princeton, NJ: ETS. (A good, clear introduction to equating.) This document is available online at: www.ets.org/Media/Research/pdf/LIVINGSTON.pdf

Livingston, S. A., & Lewis, C. (1995). Estimating the consistency and accuracy of classifications based on test scores. *Journal of Educational Measurement, 32*(2), 179–197. (The article is intended for statisticians and psychometricians, not for general readers.)

Livingston, S. A., & Zieky, M. J. (1982). *Passing scores: A manual for setting standards of performance on educational and occupational tests.* Princeton, NJ: ETS. (The first edition of this manual.)

Mills, C. N., & Jaeger, R. M. (1998). Creating descriptions of desired student achievement when setting performance standards. In L. Hansche (Ed.), *Handbook for the development of performance standards: Meeting the requirements of Title I,* (pp. 73–85).

Mitzel, H. C., Lewis, D. M., Patz, R. J., & Green, D. R. (2001). The Bookmark procedure: Psychological perspectives. In G.J. Cizek (Ed.), *Setting performance standards: Concepts, methods, and perspectives.* Mahwah, NJ: Lawrence Erlbaum Associates.

Nedelsky, L. (1954). Absolute grading for objective tests. *Educational and Psychological Measurement, 14,* 3–19. (The original description of the Nedelsky method.)

Perie, M. (2007). *A guide to understanding and developing performance level descriptors.* Dover, NH: National Center for the Improvement of Educational Assessment. Available at: www.nciea.org

Perie, M. (2007). *Setting alternate achievement standards.* Lexington, KY: University of Kentucky, Human Development Institute, National Alternate Assessment Center. This document is available online at: www.naacpartners.org/products/whitePapers/18020.pdf

Phillips, S. E. (1997). Legal defensibility of standards: Issues and policy perspectives. *Arts Education Policy Review, 98*(4), 13–19.

Plake, B. S. (2008). Standard setters: Stand up and take a stand. *Educational Measurement: Issues and Practice, 27*(1), 3-9.

Plake, B. S., & Hambleton, R. K. (2001). The Analytic Judgment method for setting standards on complex performance assessments. In G. J. Cizek (Ed.), *Standard setting: Concepts, methods, and perspectives* (pp. 283–312). Mahwah, NJ: Erlbaum.

Plake, B. S., Hambleton, R. K., & Jaeger, R. M. (1997). A new standard setting method for performance assessments: The Dominant Profile Judgment method and some field-test results. *Educational and Psychological Measurement, 57,* 400–411.

Shepard, L. A., Glaser, R., Linn, R. L., & Bohrnstedt, G. (1993). *Setting performance standards for student achievement: A report of the National Academy of Education panel on the evaluation of the NAEP Trial State Assessment: An evaluation of the 1992 achievement levels.* Stanford, CA: Stanford University, National Academy of Education. (A major criticism of question-judgment methods of setting cutscores that called these methods "fundamentally flawed" and said that the cognitive task required of the participants was almost impossible to accomplish.)

Zieky, M. (1997). Is the Angoff method really fundamentally flawed? *CLEAR Exam Review, 7*(2), 30–33. (The author's answer was "no.")

Zieky, M., & Perie, M. (2006). *A primer on setting cutscores on tests of educational achievement.* Princeton, NJ: ETS. (An overview of major issues in setting cutscores for policymakers and educators.)

GLOSSARY

Absolute Standard – A cutscore that does not depend on the distribution of the scores of the current test takers. Compare *Relative Standard.*

Accommodation – A change to a test, its administration site, its timing, its presentation mode and/or response mode to allow access to the test for a person with a disability or for an English language learner. In some usages, an *accommodation* refers to a change that does not alter the knowledge, skill, or other attribute that the test is intended to measure. In those usages, the word *modification* is used for a change that alters the knowledge, skill, or other attribute that the test is intended to measure.

Accountability Testing – The systematic and public use of test data and other information to evaluate the effectiveness of schools.

Adequate Yearly Progress (AYP) – Under the No Child Left Behind Act of 2001, the minimum level of improvement that states, school districts, and schools must demonstrate each year (as measured by the proportion of students classified as Proficient or better) to reach 100 percent Proficiency by 2014.

Alternate Achievement Standard – A separate cutscore and performance level descriptor used for special populations, typically students with significant cognitive disabilities who participate in an alternate assessment. See *Alternate Assessment.*

Alternate Assessment – A special test or other approach used in gathering information on the performance and progress of students whose attributes preclude them from valid and reliable participation in the general assessment.

Alternate Form – Different editions of a test built to the same content and statistical specifications but with different questions.

Assessment – Any systematic method of obtaining evidence from tests or other instruments to draw inferences about people or programs. In some usages, a synonym for *test*. See *Test*.

Borderline – A level of knowledge and skills that that is just barely acceptable for entry into a performance level. For example, the worst performance that is still Proficient is at the borderline for the Proficient level.

Certification – Often, the granting of advanced status by a professional organization to an applicant who demonstrates appropriately high levels of skill and ability. Sometimes used as a synonym for licensing. Compare *Licensing*.

Compensatory Scoring – Scoring a test in a way that allows high performance in one part of a test to compensate for low performance in another part of the test. A single cutscore is set for the total test, instead of separate cutscores for different parts of the test. Compare *Conjunctive Scoring*.

Conjunctive Scoring – Requiring a minimum level of performance for each separate part of the test. A separate cutscore is set for each different part of a test and each separate cutscore must be met. Compare *Compensatory Scoring*.

Consequences Data – The percents of test takers that will be classified in each performance level if a certain cutscores are used. Also called *Impact Data*. See *Performance Level*.

Constructed-Response Question – A question or exercise that requires an answer or action generated by the test taker rather than selected from a list of possible responses. Also called *Open-Ended Question* or *Free-Response Question*.

Content Standards – Statements of the knowledge and skills that students are expected to learn.

Correction for Guessing – In a multiple-choice test, the subtraction of a fraction of a point for each wrong answer to make the expected score for a test taker who guesses at random on every question equal to zero.

Criterion – Something observable that a test score is intended to predict, such as college grade point average or job performance rating.

Criterion Referenced Test – A test designed to be efficient in (1) determining the proportion of a domain of content the test taker has mastered, or in (2) determining whether or not the test taker has reached some specified level of knowledge and skills. Compare *Norm Referenced Test.*

Cutline – In the Item Descriptor Matching method, the line that a participant draws to separate the last question in a performance level from the first question in the next higher performance level. See *Performance Level.*

Cutscore – A point on a score scale at or above which test takers are classified in one way and below which they are classified in a different way. For example, if a cut score is set at 60, then people who score 60 and above may be classified as Proficient and people who score 59 and below classified as Basic.

Decision Rule – In the context of cutscores, a statement that describes how to assign test takers to performance levels based on their test scores and possibly other information. For example, a decision rule might state that scores of 60–69 result in a performance level of Basic, scores of 70–79 result in a performance level of Proficient, and scores of 80 or higher result in a performance level of Advanced. See *Performance Level.*

Equating – A statistical process used to adjust test scores so that scores on two or more alternate forms of a test can be used interchangeably. See *Alternate Form.*

Error of Measurement – In the context of testing, the difference between a test taker's score and the score that test taker would get if we could "average out" all the irrelevant factors, such as the particular questions that happen to be in a form of a test, luck in guessing, and whether the scorer (on a constructed-response question) is rigorous or lenient. See *Observed Score, Standard Error of Measurement, True Score.*

Free-Response Question – See *Constructed-Response Question.*

Impact Data – See *Consequences Data.*

Item – A test question or a specific task to be performed as part of a test.

Item Map – In the Bookmark and Item Descriptor Matching methods of setting cutscores, a listing of information about test questions in order of increasing question difficulty. Item maps typically include the number of the test question in difficulty order, the number of each question in the original test book in sequence order, the correct answer to each question, the difficulty of each question, and the content measured by each question.

Item Response Theory (IRT) – A mathematical model relating performance on test questions (items) to certain characteristics of the test takers, such as ability, and to certain characteristics of the questions, such as difficulty.

K–12 – School from Kindergarten through grade 12.

Key – The correct answer to a test question, or a listing of the correct answers to a set of test questions.

Licensing – Official permission granted by a government agency to practice an occupation or profession. Often it requires evidence that the applicant's occupational knowledge and skills are sufficient to protect the public from being endangered by allowing the applicant to practice the occupation. Compare *Certification.*

Logistic Regression – A statistical technique that yields a formula for translating one or more pieces of information (e.g., a student's test score) into the estimated probability of a specified event (e.g., a sample of the student's work being judged as proficient).

Mean – The arithmetic average of a set of numbers. The mean of a group of test scores is the sum of the scores divided by the number of scores in the group.

Median – The middle number in of a set of numbers ordered by size. If there is an even number of numbers, the median is the mean of the two middle numbers. See *Mean*.

Misclassification – The assignment of a test taker to the wrong category on the basis of a test score, as when a person who actually lacks minimal competence gets a test score high enough to pass, or when a person who is at least minimally competent fails the test.

Multiple-Choice Question – A test question in which the test taker selects the correct response from a limited number of answer choices (generally four or five). Also called a *Selected-Response Question*.

Non-disclosure Agreement – In the context of cutscores, a legal document signed by participants in a cutscore study in which they agree not to reveal the contents of confidential test questions, any confidential data, or any other confidential material.

Norm Referenced Test – A test designed to allow the scores of test takers to be compared with the scores of one or more norm groups. See *Norms*. Compare *Criterion Referenced Test*.

Norms – Test score statistics for a specified group of test takers (a "norm group"). Norms add meaning to test takers' scores by allowing comparison of a test taker's score to the scores of a specified group. For example, saying that a student's score is at the 84th percentile of a national sample of third-grade students adds meaning to the score.

Observed Score – The score a test taker obtains on a particular form of a test at a particular administration. Compare *True Score*.

Open-Ended Question – See *Constructed-Response Question*.

Operational Cutscore – A cutscore used to make decisions about people or institutions. Compare *Provisional Cutscore*.

Ordered Item Booklet – In the Bookmark and Item Descriptor Matching methods of setting cutscores, a test booklet in which the questions are ordered from easiest to most difficult with no more than one question per page.

Ordered Profile Booklet – In the Performance Profile method of setting cutscores, a collection of score profiles arranged from the lowest total score to the highest total score. See *Profile*.

P Value – The percent of test takers who answer a question correctly.

Parameter – In Item Response Theory, a number indicating a characteristic of a test question, such as its difficulty.

Participant – In this manual, a person who makes judgments about cutscores in a cutscore study. Some authors refer to participants as "judges" or "panelists."

Performance Level – A category into which test takers will be classified on the basis of their scores. The performance levels commonly used in licensure testing are Pass-Fail. The performance levels commonly used in K–12 testing are Basic, Proficient, and Advanced. Sometimes called *Proficiency Level* or *Achievement Level.*

Performance Level Descriptor – A description of what test takers must know and be able to do to be classified within a particular performance level. In K–12 educational contexts, performance level descriptors are specific to a particular subject and grade level. Often abbreviated as PLD. Also referred to as *Achievement Level Descriptor.* Compare *Policy Definition.*

Performance Standard – A definition of a level of achievement including both a minimum cutscore and a written description that distinguishes the level of achievement from other defined levels. In some usages, a performance standard is a synonym for *Cutscore.*

Performance Test – A test in which test takers actually perform tasks instead of only answering questions about how to perform them. Examples of tasks in performance tests are teaching a class, parallel parking a car, drawing a picture, performing a particular piece of music, completing a chemistry experiment, replacing a clogged fuel injector, performing an appendectomy, landing an airplane, and using a particular software package to perform some specified operations.

Policy Definition – A brief statement of the meaning of a performance level. In educational settings, performance level definitions are kept constant across grades and subjects. For example, "The Advanced level signifies performance beyond that expected of students in a grade." Compare *Performance Level Descriptor.*

Policymakers – In this manual, people who have the legal authority to decide whether or not to use cutscores and who have the legal authority to set operational cutscores for a jurisdiction.

Population – All the members of some defined group, such as third-grade students in the United States. Many populations are too large for all members of the population to be to be tested. In those cases smaller samples of members are drawn from the population. The population is the total group that a sample of people is intended to represent. Compare *Sample.*

Portfolio – A systematic collection of materials demonstrating a person's level of knowledge and skills in a particular area. For example, a writing portfolio may consist of a collection of essays written at different times on different topics; a teaching portfolio may consist of lesson plans, videotaped lessons, and original instructional materials.

Profile – A pattern of subscores on a test for a single test taker. For example, if a language arts test has subscores in reading comprehension and vocabulary, a test taker who scored higher in vocabulary than in reading comprehension would have a profile different than a test taker who scored higher in reading comprehension than in vocabulary. See *Subscore.*

Provisional Cutscore – The cutscore resulting from a cutscore study before the cutscore has been accepted by policymakers.

Regression Equation – A formula used to estimate the value of a criterion, given the value of one or more observed variables used as predictors. See *Criterion.*

Reference Group – In the context of setting cutscores, the group of test takers about which judgments are made concerning the proportion of test takers in each performance level. See *Performance Level*.

Relative Standard – A cutscore based on the test taker's score in relation to the scores of other test takers. Compare *Absolute Standard*.

Reliability – The extent to which test scores tend to be consistent, particularly across different forms of the test, and (for constructed-response tests) across different scorers.

Reliability of Classification – The extent to which classifications of test takers based on test scores (e.g., Basic vs. Proficient vs. Advanced) tend to be consistent across different forms of the test, and (for constructed-response tests) across different scorers.

Response Probability (RP) – In the Bookmark method, the given probability that a test taker at the borderline of a performance level would respond to a question correctly.

Rubric – A set of rules and guidelines for assigning scores to test takers' responses to constructed-response or performance questions. Generally, a rubric includes a description of the attributes of responses associated with each score level. Often rubrics are accompanied by examples of responses at various score levels.

Sample – A group (in testing, usually a group of people) intended to represent a larger population. For example, the 18 participants in a cutscore study may be intended to represent the thousands of teachers in a state.

Score Recipient – A person or institution to whom test scores are officially sent, either the scores of individual test takers or score statistics computed for groups of test takers.

Score Scale – The set of possible reported scores for a particular test or program.

Smoothing – Techniques for removing or reducing the irregularities in a set of numbers. One important purpose of smoothing is to replace information observed in a sample of test takers with a better estimate of the information that would have been obtained from the whole population of test takers. See *Sample, Population.*

Stakeholder – A person who is affected by the outcome of an assessment program, such as test takers, parents of minor test takers, employers, or educators.

Standard – (1) A performance standard, i.e., a required level of performance on some task along with a description of that level of performance. (2) A ruling guide or principle as in *Standards for Educational and Psychological Testing.* (3) A content standard, i.e., a statement of the knowledge and skills to be learned by students for a particular grade and subject. See *Performance Standard, Content Standards.*

Standard Deviation – A statistic that describes the amount of variation in a set of scores. The more spread out the scores, the larger the standard deviation. The standard deviation is the average distance of scores from the mean, computed by squaring those distances before averaging them and taking the square root afterward. The standard deviation is expressed in the same units as the test score. The standard deviation is the square root of the variance. Compare *Variance.*

Standard Error of Judgment – In the context of setting cutscores, a statistic commonly used to indicate the degree of disagreement in a group of participants' recommendations for the cutscore. Some common uses of the statistic assume that the participants are a random sample from the pool of all possible participants, which is rarely the case.

Standard Error of Measurement – the extent to which test scores of the same person can be expected to vary because of differences in such factors as the specific questions in different forms of the test, or the leniency or rigor of different scorers.

214

Standards for Educational and Psychological Testing – A document published by the American Educational Research Association, American Psychological Association, and National Council on Measurement in Education. It describes what these organizations officially consider necessary for appropriately developing, using, and evaluating tests. As of 2008, the latest edition of the *Standards* is 1999.

Subgroup – A part of a larger population usually defined by a characteristic such as gender, race or ethnic origin, training or formal preparation, geographic location, income level, disability, or age.

Subscore – A score derived from a subset of the questions in a test.

Test – A systematic sample of behavior taken to allow inferences about an individual's or group's knowledge, skills, or other attributes. Types of tests include multiple-choice tests, essay tests, portfolios, performance measures, structured interviews, etc.

Test Battery – A collection of tests often administered together. See *Test.*

Test Specifications – Detailed documentation of the intended characteristics of a test, including but not limited to the content and skills to be measured, the numbers and types of questions, the level of difficulty and other statistical characteristics, the timing, and the layout. See *Test.*

Threshold Region – In the context of setting cutscores using the Item Descriptor Matching method, one of the areas in an Item Map in which the performance level associated with successive items varies from a lower level to a higher level, back to a lower level, and so forth, indicating the probable location of the cutscore. See *Item Map, Performance Level.*

Trimmed Mean – The mean score computed after a specified number of the highest and lowest scores have been eliminated. See *Mean.*

True Score – The hypothetical average of the scores that a test taker would get on all the alternate forms of the test that could be made (assuming no learning or forgetting during the testing). If the scoring involves judgment, it is the average over all the forms of the test that could be made and also over all the qualified scorers who could score the test taker's responses. It is the score that a test taker would obtain if the test were perfectly reliable (i.e., if the standard error of measurement were zero). See *Alternate Form, Reliability, Standard Error of Measurement.* Compare *Observed Score.*

Validity – The extent to which inferences and actions made on the basis of a set of scores are appropriate and justified by evidence.

Variance – a statistic that describes the amount of variation in a set of scores. The variance is the square of the standard deviation. Unlike the standard deviation, the variance is **not** expressed in the same units as the scores themselves. Compare *Standard Deviation.*

Vertical Alignment – A characteristic of a set of cutscores for students in different grades being tested in the same subject. The cutscores are vertically aligned if they are appropriate when viewed as a group, without large anomalies, reversals, or unrealistic differences across grades.

Vertical Articulation – See *Vertical Alignment.*

APPENDIX

SAMPLE FORMS

This Appendix contains samples of some of the forms used in cutscore studies. You should adapt the forms for your particular needs and circumstances.

NONDISCLOSURE FORM

I understand that the test questions I will be using during the cutscore study are confidential and are the property of XXXX. I also understand that any unauthorized use, reproduction, or disclosure of these questions would be damaging to XXXX. I accept responsibility for proper use of the test questions and any other confidential materials provided to me by XXXX during the cutscore study. I agree to the following conditions:

I will return any confidential materials to XXXX upon request of an XXXX representative. I will return all confidential materials left in my possession to XXXX no later than the end of the cutscore study.

I will not copy or disclose confidential test questions or any other confidential materials provided to me by XXXX in connection with the cutscore study.

I will use the confidential questions and any other confidential materials for the sole purpose of participating in the cutscore study. I will not use the confidential questions or other confidential materials for any other purpose without the prior written permission of XXXX.

I understand that by participating in the cutscore study I do not obtain or receive any proprietary or other rights to use, reproduce, modify, or disclose the confidential questions or other confidential materials provided to me by XXXX in connection with the cutscore study.

Signed:_____

Please print your name: _____

Address: _____

_____

Date:_____

INITIAL EVALUATION OF TRAINING

The purpose of this evaluation form is to obtain your feedback about the training you have received. Your feedback will provide a basis for determining what to review before we begin the actual ratings. Please complete the information below. **Do not put your name on the form.** We want your feedback to be anonymous.

Please read each of the following statements and indicate by checking the appropriate box the degree to which you agree with each statement using the scale given (SA = Strongly Agree, A = Agree, D = Disagree, SD = Strongly Disagree).

SA A   D   SD

I understand the purpose of this workshop.

The facilitator explained things clearly.

I understand what is meant by Borderline Performance.

I understand how to make the cutscore judgment
for multiple-choice questions.

I understand how to make the cutscore judgment for
essay questions.

I understand how to use the proportion-correct
statistics (p-values).

I understand how to use the impact data.

I know what tasks to expect for the remainder of
the workshop.

I do not require any further training.

If you checked "Disagree" or "Strongly Disagree" for any of the above statements, please tell us what we need to do to better prepare you for this task. Please use the other side of the page if you need additional space.

AGREEMENT TO PROCEED

Test: _____

This is to verify that I understand how to participate in the setting of cutscores using the XXXX method. I completed the training and participated in the practice cutscore setting. Any questions that I had about setting cutscores using the XXXX method have been answered to my satisfaction. By signing this form, I state that I am ready to proceed with the process of setting cutscores using the XXXX method.

Please print your name: _____

Signature: _____

Date: _____

If you are NOT ready to proceed, please print your name above but do NOT sign the form. Please indicate below the aspects of setting cutscores by the XXXX method that are not clear to you. Use the other side of the paper if you need more space.

EVALUATION OF ROUND 1
OF THE CUTSCORE SETTING

Please place a check mark (√) in the appropriate box for each statement.

Please read each of the following statements carefully and indicate the degree to which you agree with each statement.

	Strongly Agree	Agree	Disagree	Strongly Disagree
I understood how to make the judgments.				
I understood how to use the data provided.				
I understood how to record my judgments.				
I think the process makes sense.				
I am ready to continue with round 2.				

Please indicate any areas in which you would like more information before you continue.

Please indicate any questions you may have about the remainder of the cutscore meeting.

(Use the other side of the paper if you need more space.)

EVALUATION OF THE
BOOKMARK CUTSCORE SETTING, ROUND 1

Please rate the usefulness of the following materials or procedures in placing your bookmark:	Very Useful	Somewhat Useful	Not At All Useful
Taking the test before placing a bookmark			
Reviewing the Performance Level Descriptors			
Reviewing the organization of the Ordered Item Booklet			
Receiving instruction on the Item Map			

How influential was each of the following factors in placing your bookmark?	Very Influential	Somewhat Influential	Not At All Influential
State content standards			
Performance Level Descriptors			
My perception of the difficulty of the items			
My experiences with students			
Importance of the test to the students (consequences)			

What materials, information, or procedures were most influential in your placement of the bookmark? Why?
(Use the other side of the paper if you need more space.)

FINAL EVALUATION OF THE CUTSCORE STUDY

The purpose of this final evaluation form is to obtain your feedback about the cutscore study. Your feedback will provide a basis for evaluating the training, methods, and materials. Please complete the information below. **Do not put your name on the form.** We want your feedback to be anonymous.

Gender: Male   Female

Race/ethnicity: White
African American or Black
Hispanic or Latino
American Indian or Alaska Native
Asian or Pacific Islander
Other: _____

For items 1-6, please rate each statement using the scale given in the item. Place a check mark (√) in the appropriate box for each statement.

1. Please read each of the following statements carefully and indicate the degree to which you agree with each statement.

	Strongly Agree	Agree	Disagree	Strongly Disagree
I understood the purpose of this workshop.				
The training materials contained all the information I needed to complete my assignment.				
The training in the method was adequate to give me the information I needed to complete my assignment.				
I understood how to make the judgments.				
I understood how to use the data provided.				
I understood how the cutscores were calculated.				

2. Please rate the clarity of the following instructions provided.

	Very Clear	Mostly Clear	Mostly Unclear	Very Unclear
Instructions provided in the training material				
Instructions provided by the facilitator				

3. How useful was each of the following in setting the cutscore?

	Very Useful	Somewhat Useful	Not At All Useful
Taking the test			
Practicing the cutscore procedures			
Discussion with other participants			
Cutscores of other participants			
Data on Difficulties of the questions			
Impact data (% of students in each proficiency level)			

4. How influential was each of the following in making your judgments?

	Very Influential	Somewhat Influential	Not At All Influential
Proficiency Level Descriptors			
The difficulty of the questions			
My experiences with test takers			
Definitions of borderline performance			
Discussions with other participants			
Cutscores of other participants			
Impact data (% of students in each proficiency level)			

224

5. How appropriate was the amount of time you were given to complete the different components of the cutscore study?

	Too Much Time	About Right	Too Little Time
Training on how to set cutscores			
Taking the test			
Making the first round of judgments			
Making the second round of judgments			

6. Do you believe that the final recommended cut score for each of the proficiency levels is too low, about right, or too high?

	Too Low	About Right	Too High
Basic			
Proficient			
Advanced			

7. Were there any materials or procedures that became more (or less) influential during the course of the cutscore study? If so, which ones? Why?

8. Do you have additional comments about this process or suggestions on how to improve the training and/or implementation of the cutscore study?

(Please use the other side of the page if you need more space for any response.)

EVALUATION AND RECORDING FORM
FOR AN ALIGNMENT WORKSHOP

Name _____

Signature_____ Date _____

How clear was each of the following descriptions or materials?

	Very clear	Somewhat clear	Somewhat unclear	Very unclear
The purpose of this meeting				
Your role in this meeting				
The explanation of the procedures used in the earlier cutscore study				
The use of the cutscores resulting from this meeting				
The information in the tables of cutscores				
The information in the tables of consequence data				

Please record your best recommendation for the cutscores for each assessment.

Subject	Cutscore for Proficient	Cutscore for Advanced
Grade 3 Reading		
Grade 4 Reading		
Grade 5 Reading		
Grade 3 Math		
Grade 4 Math		
Grade 5 Math		
Etc...		

For any cutscore that you changed, what influenced your recommendation? (Use the other side of the page if you need more space.)

Index

228

Index of Names

.

6777049R0

Made in the USA
Lexington, KY
19 September 2010